Patience of hope

Patience
of
hope

1 and 2 Thessalonians simply explained

J. Philip Arthur

 EVANGELICAL PRESS

EVANGELICAL PRESS
12 Wooler Street, Darlington, Co. Durham, DL1 1RQ, England

© Evangelical Press 1996
First published 1996

British Library Cataloguing in Publication Data available

ISBN 0 85234 385 X

Printed and bound in Great Britain at the Bath Press

This book is dedicated to the memory of my father,
James Leonard Arthur (1929-71),
one of whom the world was not worthy.

Lord, her watch thy church is keeping;
When shall earth thy rule obey?
When shall end the night of weeping?
When shall break the promised day?
See the whitening harvest languish,
Waiting still the labourer's toil;
Was it vain, thy Son's deep anguish?
Shall the strong retain the spoil?

Tidings sent to every creature,
Millions yet have never heard;
Can they hear without a preacher?
Lord Almighty, give the Word:
Give the Word; in every nation
Let the gospel trumpet sound,
Witnessing a world's salvation
To the earth's remotest bound.

Then the end: thy church completed,
All thy chosen gathered in,
With their King in glory seated,
Satan bound, and banished sin;
Gone for ever parting, weeping,
Hunger, sorrow, death and pain:
Lo! her watch thy church is keeping;
Come, Lord Jesus, come to reign!

Henry Downton (1818-85).

Contents

Preface

I cannot calculate the debt I owe to the members of Free Grace Baptist Church in Lancaster for their kindness in asking me to become their pastor back in 1988. In doing so they both paid me the most enormous compliment and placed a burden upon me which no mortal can ever properly discharge. I would like to acknowledge my particular indebtedness to the regulars who attend the mid-week Bible study. This book would never have been written were it not for the stimulus given by their enthusiastic and discriminating reception of a series of Bible studies on 1 and 2 Thessalonians.

While this book was in its gestation period, I picked the brains of several men who have written better books than this one. Their names, and the titles of the books in question, are mentioned in Appendix II.

I have deliberately avoided using footnotes because I set out to write for that extraordinary phenomenon known as the 'ordinary Christian'. This may mean that I have unwittingly quoted from various sources without giving proper recognition. If such quotations have crept in unawares, and are brought to my attention, I undertake to correct the matter if the book is ever reprinted. Much of the material in Appendix I is adapted from a similar appendix in *The Restoration of Israel* by Erroll Hulse of Leeds. I am grateful for his permission to lift a considerable proportion of it whole from his work and to tinker with other parts of it. Scripture quotations throughout are from the New King James Version of the Holy Scriptures, unless otherwise stated.

The staff of Evangelical Press have been enormously patient with a tardy first-time author and my wife, Barbara, has put up with me whenever I have moaned about deadlines or the wayward behaviour of a computer which sometimes shows signs of the effects of the Fall. Computers, of course, are wonderfully convenient scapegoats. Poor things, they uncomplainingly take the blame for all manner of things that are not remotely their fault. The blame for the many imperfections of this book rests with me, and with me alone! But if, in the course of time, it helps to bring one soul an inch nearer the kingdom of God, or helps one of Christ's dear children to a more complete understanding of a small portion of the vast treasure-hoard of Scripture, the effort involved in writing it will have been amply rewarded.

J. Philip Arthur
October 1996

Introduction

Who were the Thessalonians and why did the apostle Paul write two letters to them? The answer to the first question is straightforward. The Thessalonians were a group of Christians living in Thessalonica, a Greek city on the northern shore of the Aegean Sea. Nowadays it is known as Salonica and is the second-largest city in modern Greece. Paul's connection with the place dates back to the time of his second missionary journey. Together with his friend Silas, he had been travelling throughout the different provinces of Asia Minor seeking to preach the gospel and plant churches. In due course they reached the port of Troas (see Acts 16:8). At this point in his journey, Paul was undecided about his next move. He had originally intended to travel north into the province of Bithynia on the Black Sea coast of Asia Minor. This came to nothing when Paul received guidance from the Holy Spirit that God had other plans for him (Acts 16:7). Troas lay on the eastern shore of the Aegean Sea. The as yet unevangelized continent of Europe lay on the other side. This would be a tantalizing prospect for Paul who was consumed with longing to carry the gospel to regions of the world where the name of Jesus was completely unknown (Rom. 15:20). The issue was resolved when God intervened and sent Paul a vision (Acts 16:9). A man whose clothing indicated that he came from the province of Macedonia was pleading with him: 'Come over to Macedonia and help us' (Acts 16:9). What could Paul do with such a clear summons from God but obey? And what better place to start than the capital of Macedonia, the flourishing city of Thessalonica?

What kind of place was Thessalonica?

There is a brief account of Paul's visit to Thessalonica in Acts 17:1-9. A place of considerable importance, it was founded in 315 B.C. on the site of an earlier city by Cassander, an officer of Alexander the Great. He called it Thessalonica because he wished to dedicate the city to a lady of that name, the half-sister of Alexander. During the next century, Rome became the dominant power in the region and Macedonia was absorbed into the expanding Roman Empire. In the early decades of the first century B.C., the security of the Roman state was threatened by civil war. Competing generals fought to control what was then the Roman Republic. During these turbulent years, the peoples of the Empire looked on anxiously, wondering which of the rivals would come out on top. As far as Thessalonica was concerned, the outcome could not have been better. She made a wise choice and sided with the eventual victor, Augustus, who became the first Roman Emperor. This loyalty was rewarded when Thessalonica was made the capital of the province of Macedonia. It was also awarded the status of a free city and enjoyed considerable self-government under locally appointed rulers called 'politarchs'. It had a substantial harbour and was located on the main east-west highway in the region, which made it an important route centre. To Paul's mind, it was the ideal place to begin a programme of evangelism on the continent of Europe.

Paul in Thessalonica

Paul did not stay long in Thessalonica. In line with his usual practice, he began his mission by going to the synagogue of the well-established Jewish community. Altogether he spent just three Sabbaths there (Acts 17:2). His time was given over to careful and systematic exposition from the Old Testament Scriptures (note the verbs 'reasoned', 'explaining' and 'demonstrating' in Acts 17:2,3). The purpose of this exposition was to demonstrate that the 'Christ' had to 'suffer and rise again from the dead'.

Some were clearly persuaded, including Gentile 'God-fearers' and the wives of prominent members of the community (Acts 17:4). The fact that these people 'joined Paul and Silas' suggests that they became the nucleus of a church. We know the names of two of them: Aristarchus and Secundus (Acts 20:4; 27:2). This was an encouraging beginning, but it would be a mistake to suppose that these people were won round solely by Paul's eloquence. God was at work! (1 Thess. 1:5). In addition to these Gentiles who had attached themselves to the Jewish community, it is clear that a substantial number of Paul's converts had once been pagan idolaters (1 Thess. 1:9-10).

In the meantime, the other Jews, jealous of the inroads that Paul was making on their adherents, responded angrily and gathered a mob to attack the house where he was staying. It is probably a mercy that they did not find him there at the time. At any rate, they seized Jason, his host, and dragged him before the authorities, claiming that he was harbouring men who had 'turned the world upside down' (Acts 17:6). This expression is now proverbial in English. We use it when someone has caused a big stir. Paul's accusers meant much more than that. It amounts to an accusation of sedition. Paul and Silas were being accused of an attempt to topple the authorities. Although this charge was completely unfounded, the incident only ended when Jason was bound over to keep the peace (Acts 17:9), which meant that he had to guarantee that Paul would not return to Thessalonica. No doubt some harsh penalty would have been imposed on Jason if Paul had come back. This would go a long way to explain why Paul, ejected after a comparatively short stay in Thessalonica, felt that he could not return (1 Thess. 2:18).

Why study 1 Thessalonians?

This epistle vies with Galatians for the claim to be the earliest portion of the New Testament to have been written. Its value to the modern Christian is closely tied in with Paul's reasons for writing it. It seems likely that he was writing from Corinth, somewhere in the period A. D. 51-53. His stay in Thessalonica had been brief. He obviously felt very keenly the fact that he had not been able to give the believers the depth of instruction that they needed. In addition, his departure had been occasioned by an outburst of persecution. Was the infant church standing up to it? Furthermore, 'a great multitude' (Acts 17:4) had professed faith. Had it all been a flash in the pan? In order to alleviate his concerns, Paul had sent Timothy to Thessalonica to see how things stood. The news had been reassuring, so much so that Paul expressed himself in an exuberant way: 'Now we really live' (1 Thess. 3:8, NIV). Nevertheless, Timothy's report made it clear that problems needed to be addressed. In the way that he dealt with these problems, Paul has left the church in all ages with teaching ideally suited for Christians facing a number of challenges.

1. It is an epistle for all who are concerned about evangelism

The church in Thessalonica was having to deal with a whispering campaign. Paul himself was the object of the attack. Jewish opponents of the church hoped to undermine it by denigrating his character. Among other things, they alleged that he was trying to make money out of the believers (2:9). It also seems that they made capital out of the fact that Paul had not returned to Thessalonica (2:18). On the face of it, this laid the apostle open to the charge that he had abandoned his friends. Paul's approach was to tackle this head-on (chapters 1 and 2). He took great pains to defend himself against the accusations of his detractors. From the point of view of the modern Christian, this is invaluable. We have a priceless opportunity to find out what made Paul tick, to look into the heart of the man and discover the burning passion for Christ and his gospel which made him the man that he was. If we have any concern to see other people brought to faith in Christ, we could not do better than take a good look at Paul. He is a superb role-model for any Christian who wants to be a committed yet responsible evangelist.

2. It is an epistle for all who are concerned about the last things

Some members of the church were puzzled. What was going to happen when God finally brought the affairs of this world to a conclusion? They knew that Jesus had promised to come back, but what would be the nature of his return and how would it affect those who had already fallen asleep? (4:13). Paul's response (4:13 - 5:11), taken together with further teaching on the same theme in 2 Thessalonians 2:1-12, has left us with two of the clearest statements in the whole New Testament about the Second Coming of Christ and the end of the age. Every chapter in 1 Thessalonians ends with a reference to the Second Coming!

3. It is an epistle for all who want to live well for Jesus

Many of the converts in Thessalonica had come to Christ from a pagan background. They needed help to appreciate the demands of their new-found faith. Paul was concerned to leave them in no doubt about implications of holiness in such areas as sexual morality and the need to live an orderly life that would not bring the gospel into disrepute (4:1-12; 5:12-28). Because we live in a post-Christian society, it is increasingly likely that we shall see people brought to faith in Christ who have not been exposed to much Christian teaching or to Christian morality. Like the young converts in first-century Thessalonica, they will emerge from a background of religious pluralism and a moral climate where anything goes. We cannot take it for granted that people like that will automatically know how to live for God. If the next generation of converts is to be effective, it will need to give serious attention to Paul's counsel to young believers in Thessalonica twenty centuries ago.

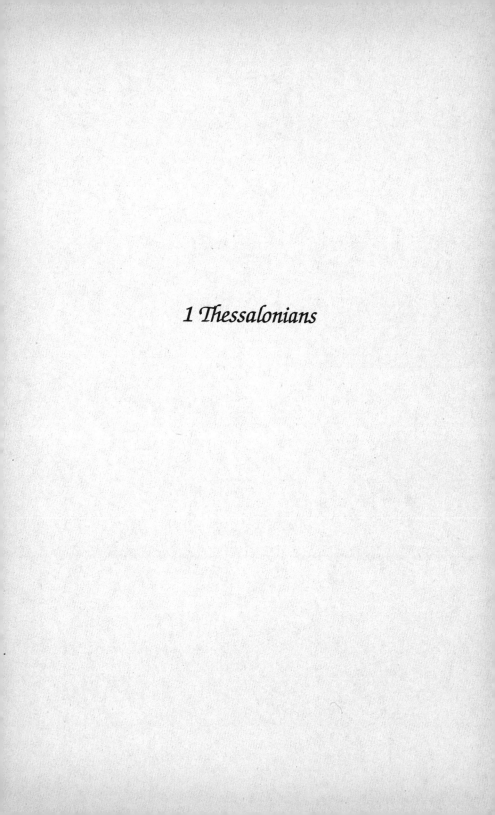

1 Thessalonians

1.
Paul greets the Thessalonians

Please read 1 Thessalonians 1:1-4

Paul's greeting (1:1)

When I see a letter on the doormat, the first thought that crosses my mind is: 'Who is it from?' Sometimes the hand-writing on the envelope will tell me. If it comes from a part of the country where I don't know many people, the postmark may provide a clue to the identity of the sender. But if the franking is blurred, I may have to rely on the address at the top of the letter. Nevertheless, I often find I have to turn to the end of the letter before my curiosity is satisfied and I can begin reading it. If all else fails, I can expect to find the name of my correspondent there. In the ancient world, things were done differently. Letters usually began with the name of the sender, which is why Paul wrote his name before he wrote anything else. Two other names are mentioned, those of Silas, who is called by the Latin form of his name, Silvanus, and Timothy. These two men had worked alongside Paul during his stay in Thessalonica.

It was also a convention of first-century letter-writing to include a prayer, seeking the blessing of the gods on the recipient. No doubt a considerable measure of tact was some-times involved in remembering which of the many deities available was the favourite of the individual concerned. The apostle, however, did not need to ransack the enormous catalogue of pagan gods to find a point of contact with his readers. Instead, he expressed his desire that they might enjoy grace and peace **'from God our Father and the Lord Jesus Christ'**.

In writing as he did, Paul echoed the conventional form of words in use at the time. Instead of the Greek word for 'greeting' he used a similar-sounding word which means 'grace'. To this he added the Greek version of the familiar Jewish greeting, *'Shalom'*, or 'Peace'. This was much more than mere formal politeness. Grace and peace are two of the loveliest words in the Christian vocabulary.

Grace is the undeserved favour of God, his kindness to those who merit his wrath and condemnation. Human sinfulness means that we are entitled to feel the weight of divine anger against sin. What a relief to know that God is merciful! Grace prompted him to send his Son into the world to live and die in the place of sinners.

Peace follows naturally on from grace. Because God is gracious, it is gloriously possible for those who have offended him to be reconciled to him. Where once there were enmity and estrangement, now there is peace, and since God no longer has a quarrel against his people, they can be at peace within and among themselves. It follows that the word 'peace' involves more than the absence of war: it includes what Leon Morris calls 'a flourishing state of soul'.

Paul's friends in Thessalonica had already experienced the grace of God in their lives, together with the peace which flows from it. Had this not been the case, they would not have been Christians at all. Nevertheless, it was his earnest longing that they might enjoy these blessings to a much greater degree.

The church of the Thessalonians (1:1-4)

Paul clearly had a good memory. It seems that he was in the habit of praying for his friends in Thessalonica in a disciplined and conscientious way. He prayed for them all. No one was left out. We learn something of the content of his prayers for them later in the epistle (3:11-13), but at this stage the dominant thought in his mind was thanksgiving. He was very grateful to God that his saving mercy had brought these people into his life. For what did the apostle give thanks? There were certain qualities evident in the lives of these believers which showed that God was at work. In this respect, the church at Thessalonica was typical of every local gathering of believers ever since.

1. A church rooted in God

The believers in Thessalonica could have been excused if they had felt that their situation was precarious. The church was a few months old at most. Unlike many churches today, there was no core of experienced members who could provide maturity and stability. There had been little time to acquire a grasp of Christian teaching or to come to terms with the demands of Christian behaviour. They were still raw recruits. Moreover they faced the additional pressures of being denied access to Paul himself, combined with persecution from the wider community. It would have been very tempting to have been seized by pessimism.

How could a handful of inexperienced believers, ignorant of the finer points of doctrine and still adjusting to their new Christian lifestyle, hope to weather the storm of persecution? Paul understood that it would certainly help if they could acquire a firm grasp of their true identity. This explains his choice of words in verse 1. They were not merely the church in Thessalonica; they were a church **'in God the Father and the Lord Jesus Christ'**.

The word **'church'** is itself highly significant. The way in which it is used in everyday speech is rather confusing. Most people use it to describe a building where religious services are held. ('Turn left just after the parish church.') Paul had something else in mind. He used a Greek word which referred to a gathering of people who had assembled for some shared purpose. His friends had come together because they had something in common.

Each one knew what it meant to be 'in God' and 'in Jesus Christ'. This is rich terminology. We first meet it in John 15:1-8, where Jesus pictured his disciples as the branches of a vine. He, of course, is the vine and the branches are in him and must continue to draw their life from him. In similar fashion, Paul himself describes Christians as being 'in Christ' in the same way that limbs and organs are part of a human body (Rom. 12:5). Both ideas, the branches of the vine and the parts of the body, do more than say that believers belong to God. They make the point that the relationship between God and his people is extraordinarily close. They share in his life. While it was undoubtedly true that the Christians in Thessalonica were green and untried, they still had considerable grounds for encouragement. Had not the Lord himself identified with them in the closest measure? In the same way, modern believers facing an uphill struggle can comfort themselves with the thought that though they may be very weak, God is committed to them and will no more discard them than a mighty oak would jettison one of its branches or a strong man his right arm.

2. A church characterized by faith, love and hope

One of the most impressive aspects of Paul's service for Christ was his prayer life. His friends in Thessalonica were a small fraction of a numerous company of people who never left his thoughts. His prayers for them were marked by a deep sense of thanksgiving (1:2-4). He rejoiced with gratitude because certain qualities were evident in their lives. Three qualities stood out, and these are as essential for the well-being of a church now as they were then. They are faith, love and hope.

Faith. A true church is made up of people who have faith in Jesus Christ. People without such faith are not Christians, and any collection of individuals without it, however religious they might be, is not a church. Faith includes the idea of confidence; it is convinced that Jesus can be trusted. I can rightly claim to have such faith if I am confident that a holy God will accept his sinless life in place of my lifetime of moral failure. I can rest assured that when the Son of God died at Calvary, he took my place, willingly enduring the wrath of God so that I need not do so. The Christians at Thessalonica had entrusted their eternal well-being to the Lord of glory, convinced that he loved them and had given himself for them (Gal. 2:20). Do you have faith? Be assured that no one will ever ask you a more important question. You can answer in the affirmative if you have entrusted all that you are to all that Jesus is, if you are relying upon his life and death in the place of sinners to atone for your sins and secure your peace with God.

Paul thanked God for his friends in Thessalonica because their faith was *productive.* He spoke of their **'work of faith'**. Paul was often in the habit of contrasting faith and works. It was necessary that he should, for the human heart has a persistent tendency to seize hold of the idea that we can work our way into the favour of God. Nevertheless, true faith is not sterile, but active. Elsewhere, Paul said that it works 'through love' (Gal. 5:6). James tells us that 'Faith by itself, if it does not have works, is dead' (James 2:17). He went on to insist that the only solid proof that a person truly has faith in God is his life of obedience to God (James 2:18).

Love. A true church is made up of people who love God and who love one another. The apostle John tells us that the person who does not love in this way 'does not know God' (1 John 4:8). This is because love of this kind does not arise naturally in the human heart. Until we are transformed by the grace of God, we are incapable of it. When such love is present, it is the response of a renewed heart to the love of God. 'We love him because he first loved us' (1 John 4:19). The love of Christ for his people brought him from the glory of heaven to the squalor of Bethlehem's stable, kept him steadfast throughout a life of sorrow and delivered him up to the horror of Calvary, a horror that included not only wounds and bleeding, hunger and thirst, but also the undiluted wrath of God against the sin of his people. Who could not love him in return? The fact that some people cannot find it in themselves to do so is a sad commentary on the hardness of human hearts.

It also needs to be observed that when the love of God is shed abroad in a believer's heart (Rom. 5:5), there will be love for other Christians. In the first place, it is a moral necessity: 'If God so loved us, we also *ought* to love one another' (1 John 4:11, emphasis added). Secondly, when a person who claims to have a stake in the love of Christ cannot find it in himself to love other believers, it poses a question about his genuineness: 'He who does not love his brother whom he has seen, how can he love God whom he has not seen?' (1 John 4:20).

When Paul thanked God for the love that was evident in the lives of his brothers and sisters in Thessalonica, he was not referring to something abstract and insubstantial but something tough and practical. He wrote about their **'labour of love'**. This expression has a slightly different meaning in modern English from the one that Paul intended. Nowadays, a labour of love is a generous action performed purely for the sake of it. Many a man gives up an evening or two a week to coach a boys' football team for no other reason than that he enjoys doing so! The love that Paul had in mind, however, was the self-giving love that characterizes God himself, the love that reached out to us 'while we were still sinners' (Rom. 5:8). In effect, the believers in Thessalonica had begun to imitate the Saviour. Both within the church and outside it, they were making a determined effort to love the unlovely and to do so with strenuous exertion.

Hope. Like faith and love, hope is an essential component of the make-up of every true believer. Once again we need to recognize the fact that the word 'hope', as we use it in everyday English, does not really convey what Paul intended. Nowadays the word has a speculative ring to it. 'Shall we have a white Christmas this year? I hope so!' The person who says such things means that he is not certain how things will turn out, but feels optimistic. Our modern usage of the word is neatly summed up in that sarcastic remark that 'Marriage is a triumph of hope over experience.' Here is a person who ought to know better, but in spite of the evidence of failed marriages all around him, retains his sunny optimism that his wedding day will usher in a lifetime of shared happiness!

Paul had something very different in view. It was his conviction that the Christian can anticipate a golden future with complete confidence. It is not a matter of likelihood or probabilities but of absolute certainty. Jesus will return and make all things new. The matter is not in doubt. Michael Faraday, the eminent Victorian physicist, made no secret of his Christian faith. While he lay on his deathbed, he was chided: 'Where are your speculations now, Michael?' 'Speculations?', he retorted, 'I'm dealing in certainties!' The same mood had gripped the believers in first-century Thessalonica.

This hope of theirs was *patient*. The patience in question is not the resignation of the stoic, the 'grit your teeth and get on with it' attitude of the person who likes to appear completely unmoved by adverse circumstances. The Christian anticipates the return of his Saviour with calm confidence. Buoyed up by this hope, he can endure the shocks of life in a resilient and cheerful spirit. Whatever things might be like in the short term, it will all turn out well in the end.

3. A church chosen by God

Like all the people of God in every era of Christian history, the men and women who made up the fellowship in Thessalonica had been chosen by God. The word **'election'** simply means choice. No more than five years may pass in the United Kingdom without a general election being held so that those people who are entitled to vote can say whom they would prefer to represent them in Parliament. A nationwide secret ballot ensures that the choice of the majority is respected in each constituency. The biblical doctrine of election simply means that God ordains to eternal life all who come to faith in Christ (Acts 13:48). He did so 'before the foundation of the world' for no other reason than the 'good pleasure of his will' (Eph. 1:4,5). Election, however, is not arbitrary, a random choice along the lines of 'Eeny-meeny-miny-mo'. While God saves those whom he is pleased to save, he does so because he loves them. This is not to say that he loves and therefore chooses certain people because they are worthy of it. No one deserves the electing love of God. Christians are not chosen because they are holy. They are chosen in order that they might become holy (Eph. 1:4).

Some believers appear to be very nervous when they are confronted with the Bible's teaching on this subject, as though they fear that their repentance from sin and faith in Christ might all turn out to be futile because, in spite of it all, they were not among the secret number of the elect. No Christian need ever give way to such fears. Paul said that he knew that his friends in Thessalonica were chosen by God. He knew it, not because he had secret access to the heavenly equivalent of classified information, but because election has consequences. Chosen people exhibit faith, love and hope. No one who has entrusted himself to the mercy of Christ, who finds himself overwhelmed with a sense of love and gratitude to God for all that Jesus has achieved and who looks forward with longing to the Saviour's return will ultimately find that none of this counted for anything because the mystery of divine election had passed him by. His faith in Christ, love for Christ and confident expectation that Christ will come again as he has promised are proof positive that he is among the chosen of God.

2.
The impact of the gospel

Please read 1 Thessalonians 1:5-10

Paul's prayer of thanksgiving for all that God had accomplished in the lives of his friends is followed by an assessment of the impact of the gospel upon them. His prayer provided us with an opportunity to consider certain features of a true church. It is appropriate that he should move on to examine the gospel, for gospel and church are inextricably bound up with one another. The church comes into being when the gospel is proclaimed, yet the call to proclaim the gospel is the responsibility of the church.

The Thessalonians' response to the gospel (1:5-8)

The gospel is a force to be reckoned with; it is dynamic. This is partly the thinking behind Paul's choice of verb: the gospel 'came' (1:5). It was not so much a product which Paul and Silas delivered, but a power in its own right. Paul and Silas were the servants of a living, vital energy. The gospel is not merely a set of ideas which depend for their effectiveness on the persuasiveness of the messenger. When the Christian message is proclaimed it involves a verbal presentation of truth, but over and beyond that, the gospel is itself an agent of divine power (cf. Rom. 1:16). The role of the Holy Spirit is of critical importance. It was because he was at work that the gospel had such impetus in Thessalonica. His power was responsible for the 'assurance', the conviction in the hearts not only of Paul and Silas, but also of the hearers themselves, that their message came from God. Is there an evangelist today who would not be thrilled to see the same evidence of the Holy Spirit at work? Nevertheless, we need to recognize that the sovereign Spirit of God cannot be domesticated. He does not come and go at our beck and call. 'The wind blows where it wishes' (John 3:8). All that we can do is to plead with God for a great outpouring of his Spirit. The response is a matter for his sovereign pleasure. But given that we have no control over the activity of the Holy Spirit, we can enhance the credibility of our message by ensuring that our own character does not undermine the truth we proclaim. This is why Paul reminded his friends about **'what kind of men'** he, Silas and Timothy had been when they were in Thessalonica (1:5). This is not a case of self-promotion, but a recognition that God had enabled them to live lives that were in tune with the message they preached.

The gospel had made phenomenal progress. Three stages can be observed. First of all, the gospel 'came' to the Thessalonians (1:5). They in turn gave it an enthusiastic reception (1:6). It met with a hearty welcome. Then, in third place, these brand-new Christians became enthusiastic advocates for the gospel which they had received: **'The word of the Lord ... sounded forth'** (1:8). This expression suggests something dramatic, a trumpet-blast or even a thunderclap. The believers in Thessalonica published the good news to such effect that it was audible over a wide swathe of territory. Macedonia and Achaia were the two Roman provinces that covered the bulk of modern Greece (1:8,9). The results of their energetic witness were so impressive that Paul felt that he could say, **'We do not need to say anything'** (1:8). It is difficult to imagine the great apostle ever falling silent about the message of salvation, but it must have encouraged the believers in Thessalonica to know that he clearly felt heartened by the verve they had shown in publishing the message of the cross. Modern Christians would do well to learn from their example. So often, nowadays, the task goes by default.

Young as they were in the faith, the Thessalonian Christians had learned, like Paul himself, that nothing cripples evangelism more effectively than hypocrisy. We find that they had not only made heroic efforts to pass on the verbal message of the gospel, but they had also worked hard to embody that message in their lives. The Thessalonians became **'followers'** (1:6). This translates a Greek word which can also be rendered 'imitators' (it actually lies behind the English word 'mimic'). They set out to copy Paul and in doing so, copied Jesus in turn. The imitators became **'examples'** (1:7). They, in their turn, became impressive advertisements for the transforming power of grace, even though the circumstances in which they began to copy Paul and Silas were far from encouraging.

The nature of the **'affliction'** is detailed for us in the account in Acts 17:1-9. That is why Paul is careful to note that the joy they showed can only be explained supernaturally. The change in the Thessalonian believers was so marked that it became a topic of conversation over a wide area. Paul delighted to talk about the faith of his friends, but in one sense this was quite unnecessary: everybody already knew about it; other people told Paul. Is this an area where the people of God living towards the close of the second millennium can afford to feel comfortable with their performance? How do we compare with our spiritual ancestors of two thousand years ago?

The gospel to which the Thessalonians responded (1:9-10)

In describing the change which came upon the Christians in Thessalonica, Paul has provided his readers then and now with a graphic picture of conversion. He traces three distinct elements.

1. They turned away from idols

This tells us immediately that the bulk of Paul's first readers were converts from paganism rather than from a Jewish background. The idols in question will have been images of a tangible and obvious kind, man-made statues intended to represent the deities who were supposed to reside on Mount Olympus. Turning in faith to the living God necessarily involved repudiating their former allegiance to such vanities. At various times in history, Christianity has come into collision with idol-worship of this kind.

Early in the eighth century, an Englishman named Boniface, who was born near Crediton in Devon, went as a missionary to the German lands. At Geismar in Hesse he challenged the power of the pagan gods by hewing down a giant oak tree sacred to the worship of Thor and using its timber to construct a chapel.

In the middle years of the sixteenth century, the interior of many parish churches in England underwent a radical transformation when statues and pictures depicting Jesus, Mary and the saints were destroyed. Nowadays, spokesmen for the heritage industry argue that this was wanton vandalism, that priceless works of art were lost for ever because of mindless bigotry. In many cases, however, the destruction of images sprang from the purest of motives. The Reformation had brought about a rediscovery of the gospel and a renewed commitment to the teaching of Scripture in all its broad scope. God is not to be worshipped through the use of carved images (Exod. 20:4-6). The fact that Roman Catholic and Eastern Orthodox use of such images has gained respectability because it is a custom with the weight of centuries behind it is nothing to the point. The Reformers and Puritans cleared such objects out of their church buildings precisely because of their respect for the living God.

Even today, Christian missionaries still encounter idolatry of this crude and obvious kind, where images of wood and stone, or natural features — rivers, rocks and trees — are regarded as repositories of spiritual power.

Idol-worship, however, can be much more subtle. In the wider sense, an idol is a God-substitute. The fallen imagination is so fertile that human beings down the centuries have invented thousands of idols: the number of things that a person may put in God's place is legion. The Chinese people who run the take-away restaurant near my home have an image of the kitchen god on a shelf, but while most other folk in my overwhelmingly white neighbourhood would not have anything of that sort in their homes, they are idol-worshippers for all that. Some make an idol of a career, others of their home. The fast car, the hi-fi equipment or personal stereo, or for that matter any other lifestyle accessory, can easily be promoted in the mind of its owner to the status of deity. How many people treat another person, a husband, or wife, girlfriend or boyfriend, parent or child, as only God deserves to be treated? It also needs to be said that when they seek an object of worship, many people look no further than themselves. To become a Christian is to turn one's back on the old life of self-pleasing and self-satisfaction. In that sense, every convert to the faith of Jesus turns away from idols.

> The dearest idol I have known,
> Whate'er that idol be!
> Help me to tear it from thy throne,
> And worship only thee.

2. *They began to serve the living and true God*

There is a double movement involved in conversion. As well as turning *away from sin and self*, those who are converted turn *to God*.

Paul makes a twin contrast between the service of God and the folly of idol-worship. To begin with, *God is alive; the idols are not.* The psalmist described the idols of his own time as objects of ridicule:

> They have mouths, but they do not speak;
> Eyes they have, but they do not see;
> They have ears, but they do not hear;
> Noses they have, but they do not smell;
> They have hands, but they do not handle;
> Feet they have, but they do not walk;
> Nor do they mutter through their throat
>
> (Ps. 115:5-7).

He followed this with the sad observation that those who make such lifeless images are every bit as dead as they are (Ps. 115:8). God is so great that nothing and no one may fitly be compared to him. Idols of all descriptions, whether religious statues or something less obvious, are cheap and tawdry substitutes for the glorious Monarch of the universe. The Christian is a spiritual realist. He devotes his life to the service of one who is worthy of it.

Secondly, *the living God is true; the idols are false.* Those who serve them devote their lives to promoting a lie. The true God, however, is the one who has revealed himself to mankind in the Bible. For some years we lived next to an old Jewish lady. I once remember her looking on approvingly as we took our children to church. 'It's good for children to have a

religion,' she said. Presumably she thought that it was good
from the point of view of social cohesion. Any religion would
do so long as it gave youngsters an awareness of their cultural
heritage and a sense of right and wrong. Paul's friends in
Thessalonica already had religion. What they lacked was
Christ. They turned to the God who sent his Son into the world
to save sinners, the God who has reconciled himself to erring
mankind through the death of his Son. They turned to the God
and Father of our Lord Jesus Christ and to no other. To become
a Christian is not to turn to piety, religion, or even some god
or other, but to turn to the God who, in the person of Jesus
Christ, is the way, the truth and the life (John 14:6).

3. They were waiting for the Son of God

The believers in Thessalonica had begun to serve the living
and true God. Like John Wesley, they wanted to be 'up and
doing for Jesus'. This activity, however, was coupled with a
patient realization that all will not be finally put to rights until
Jesus returns in power and great glory to make all things new.
This world of ours is so thoroughly permeated by sin that it
cannot be mended by mere human effort. Our ultimate hope
for a just society does not rest in the heroic labours of Christian
people in the present but in the intervention of the Son of God
at the end of time.

When Jesus does return, he will save his people from the
wrath to come. We have no right to try to soften the force of
such statements. The wrath of God is a necessary consequence
of his justice. He cannot overlook moral evil but must punish
those who are guilty. In what sense is Jesus a saviour at all, if
rebellious men and women will not receive the due reward for
their deeds? What is there to be saved from if hell does not
exist?

3.
Paul's conduct in Thessalonica

Please read 1 Thessalonians 2:1-16

In chapters 2 and 3 of his epistle, Paul sets out to defend his conduct during his stay in Thessalonica. This was not prompted by vanity or a desire to promote himself. There was too much at stake for that kind of empty posturing. As a servant of the gospel, Paul knew that the credibility of the message that he preached depended on the credibility of its messengers. His opponents understood this only too well. If they could succeed in their attempt to undermine his character, this would have the effect of bringing down the gospel too. No one would take the Christian message seriously if it could be proved that its chief missionary was a money-grubbing fraud with suspect motives. The future of the gospel in Thessalonica was at stake. It was vital that the apostle should answer the false accusations of his enemies. To begin with, he reviewed his behaviour during the short period that he was actually present in Thessalonica (2:1-16). His opponents had made considerable capital out of his sudden departure, so he went on to explain why that had been necessary, along with his repeated but frustrated attempts to return.

Paul's genuineness (2:1-6)

When Paul and his fellow-missionaries arrived in Thessalonica, they did not come **'in vain'**. This translates a Greek phrase which means 'empty'. Naturally this prompts the question: 'Empty of what?' Did he mean that his time there was not empty of success, that it was not a failure? After all, there was ample evidence that the power of God was at work (1:5). If this was Paul's intended meaning, it was no more than the truth. It seems likely, however, that he had something else in mind. Verse 2 opens with the word 'but', which suggests that Paul wanted to make a contrast. In spite of all that had taken place in Philippi, he came to Thessalonica nothing daunted. His resolve to preach the gospel had not been shaken by the humiliating treatment that he had received. He did not simply arrive in Thessalonica because it was a port in a storm, a convenient place to hole up and lick his wounds. He was not a piece of human flotsam washed up in Macedonia by the tide of events. There was a purpose behind it all. He came as a man with a mission.

This tells us a great deal about the apostle's calibre. While in Philippi, he and his friend Silas had been subjected to a brutal public beating with the added humiliation of having been stripped naked. This was followed by imprisonment and confinement in the stocks (Acts 16:22-24). As this was by no means the first time that such treatment had been meted out to him, Paul deserves our admiration for his willingness to risk similar persecution all over again. Every new attempt to proclaim the gospel would involve him in an internal battle where he would have to face and conquer his fears. At different times in the history of Christianity, the same impressive persistence has been the hallmark of evangelists and missionaries. George Whitefield once said that broken heads and dead cats were 'honourable badges', 'the ornaments of a methodist'. (At that time, the word 'methodist' was not the label of a particular denomination. It was commonly applied to any enthusiastic Christian.) We must not miss Paul's insistence that he was not naturally courageous. His boldness was God-given. Even so, it was powerful additional evidence of his genuineness. Here was a man who had often suffered in the past and who knew that more suffering of the same kind would come his way in the future. Nevertheless, he kept on going. This was hardly the behaviour of a charlatan!

Accusations against Paul (2:3)

Three accusations appear to have been levelled at Paul:

1. His message was 'deceitful'

His rivals claimed that Paul was not on the side of the truth, but a dealer in lies, a purveyor of falsehoods. His response to this was that the gospel that he preached was not something that he had dreamed up, but something that had been entrusted to him by God himself (2:4). It is often said that Paul was an innovator, that he had imposed a number of modifications on the message of Jesus Christ. His own view of his mission was very different. His image of himself at this point is that of the steward, someone charged with the responsibility of guarding the property of his master. Paul stood by the trustworthiness of his message, because ultimately it did not originate with him at all, but in the mind of the Almighty.

Elsewhere, the apostle insisted that he and his colleagues had 'renounced the hidden things of shame, not walking in craftiness nor handling the word of God deceitfully, but by manifestation of the truth' he commended himself to 'every man's conscience in the sight of God' (2 Cor. 4:2). No modern evangelist can afford to be any different.

2. His message was 'unclean'

This translates a word that can also be rendered 'impure'. It has sometimes been argued that this was an allegation that Paul had behaved unwisely in his relations with the opposite sex. 'Not a few of the leading women' had been converted in Thessalonica (Acts 17:4). Perhaps his detractors saw an ulterior motive at work: 'Your wives and daughters are not safe with this man!' Spiritual leaders exercise a position of trust and, down the years, many have abused it. The predatory behaviour of high-profile televangelists has been a gift to muck-raking journalists in recent years and many of us have had the grief of observing colleagues in the gospel ministry fall prey to sexual temptation and so bring the name of God into disrepute (Rom. 2: 24). Even so, it seems probable that the accusation levelled at Paul was more general in its scope, namely that he was not sincere, that his motives were questionable. His answer was that he had the approval of the Almighty (2:4). Over the years, he had proved himself worthy of the trust reposed in him. Whatever the insinuations of his critics, his track record had satisfied the most demanding judge of all.

3. His message was characterized by 'guile'

In the same way that a fisherman baits his hook with an enticing lure, it was alleged that Paul had set out to gain converts by trickery. There have always been unscrupulous evangelists who gain adherents by painting a dazzling picture of the Christian life which is attractive precisely because it conveniently ignores the true cost of discipleship. Paul's response was that he had never tailored his words to suit his hearers because he was concerned to pass the scrutiny of God himself (2:4-5). Continually aware that all his actions were carried out under the unwavering gaze of a holy God, the apostle was concerned to please him. This freed him from the temptation to say only what would please his listeners.

To sum up, Paul was altogether free of ulterior motives. The Thessalonian believers could rest assured that he neither wanted their money, nor their approval. Admiration, whether theirs or anyone else's, was not the prize that he sought (2:6). This raises him far above the normal plane of saved humanity. The good opinion of our fellows is seductive. The desire to be well thought of is a powerful drug. How many of us can truly claim to be immune to it?

Paul's refusal to accept financial support (2:6-9)

One issue that shows Paul's conduct in its true light is his approach to the question of financial support (2:6-9). It proved beyond a shadow of a doubt that he was not 'in it for the money'. The religious scene of the first century was populated by a mass of itinerant philosophers, teachers and wise men who hawked their pet insights from place to place and made a fat living in the process. Paul's opponents tried to neutralize his effectiveness by spreading the slur that he was no better than the rest — just one more swindler exploiting the natural respect of ordinary folk for religion. Paul's answer to this charge deserves to be examined with some care. On the one hand, there is a spirited repudiation of the charge that he was a charlatan ruthlessly seeking to part decent people from their cash. Equally, it would be wrong to conclude from his argument here that there is no place for a paid ministry in the Christian church. There is a clear statement here to the effect that he would have been within his rights to have made **'demands'** on them (2:6). Elsewhere, Paul argued that it is just and proper for those who perform spiritual work to receive material support from the churches (1 Cor. 9:3-16). He himself 'took wages' from other churches while engaged in ministry at Corinth (2 Cor. 11:8) and was grateful for the gift sent by the church at Philippi (Phil. 4:10-20). His overriding principle, as with so many other issues, was that 'All things are lawful to me, but all things are not expedient' (1 Cor. 6:12, AV). When he went to Thessalonica, he judged it appropriate to abstain from this entitlement because that would free him from the charge of covetousness. In the event, that very accusation was levelled at him! At other times he fell foul of the opposite, but equally irrational, accusation that his refusal to insist on his right to financial maintenance was simply a ploy to achieve an undeserved reputation for humility! (2 Cor. 11:7).

In the event, Paul's decision to support his ministry by working at his own trade (he was a tentmaker — Acts 18:3) must have cost him a great deal in terms of exhaustion and unremitting effort. The phrase **'labour and toil'** translates a rhyming pun in the Greek which could be rendered 'moiling and toiling'. The idea is that between his evangelism and his tent-making, he had no time to call his own. Always at full stretch, he must have been permanently drained. The one charge that could not be made to stick was the ludicrous notion that he was cynically trying to enrich himself. The Thessalonian Christians knew this for a fact: they had seen him at work (2:10).

Circumstances vary enormously from place to place and from one period of history to another. The rural clergy who figure in Anthony Trollope's novels of nineteenth-century England lived at a time when a bishop could reward a compliant underling by appointing him to a good 'living', a parish with generous revenues which would guarantee a lifetime of leisured affluence. Evangelical ministers in modern Britain, however, are not noted for high levels of income. At the other end of the scale, American televangelists have become a byword for prodigal wealth. Covetousness is a two-edged sword. Whatever our means, we are never free of it. In the United Kingdom at least, no one would enter the ministry in order to line his pockets, but he may well fight a battle with covetousness for the whole of his time in it because of his relative poverty. However, it should never be assumed that a higher level of income will free us from that insidious desire to want more. At this point, Paul is a challenge to every Christian in our materialistic age. How many of us could say with complete candour what he says in Philippians 4:11-13: 'Not that I speak in regard to need, for I have learned in whatever state I am, to be content: I know how to be abased, and I know how to abound. Everywhere and in all things I have learned both to be full and to be hungry, both to abound and to suffer need. I can do all things through Christ who strengthens me'?

As well as the particular matter of his refusal to demand financial support, these verses also show us much about Paul's general outlook while he was in Thessalonica. His whole treatment of the believers there had been characterized by gentleness (2:7). There is some support for the idea that Paul even meant to say that he had been as tender as a baby. (In Greek there is only the difference of one letter between the words 'baby' and 'gentle'. Some of the older manuscripts use the first. Equally some commentators hesitate. Would Paul really have intended to compare himself both to an infant child and **'a nursing mother'** in the same sentence?) At any rate, no one could justly accuse the apostle of throwing his weight about. Far from treating the whole exercise as a 'power trip', he was gentleness personified.

In addition, some of Paul's detractors might well have portrayed him as a sinister, manipulative individual: 'He's out to get you!' (An old lady of my acquaintance once warned her granddaughter to have nothing to do with Baptists: 'You'll get roped in. They're ever so good at roping people in!') At this point, the apostle admitted that he was guilty as charged (2:8). It is as though he said, 'I do want you. Indeed I ache for you, but that is because I want to give you something.' There were in fact two things that the apostle wanted to share with his friends: the gospel and his own life. These people mattered to him!

Paul's appeal to the Thessalonians' own recollection of things (2:10-16)

Paul invited his friends to think back. Could they not remember for themselves? Note the repetition: **'You are witnesses'** (2:10), **'you know...'** (2:11). Again his main emphasis was that he had behaved like a father. Who could matter more to a father than his own offspring? Paul reassured the Thessalonian Christians that he saw his relationship with them in exactly those terms. Like any responsible parent, he wanted the best for his children, namely that they would live a life **'worthy of God who calls you into his own kingdom and glory'**.

Was Paul genuine? His words in verse 13 are an invitation to the believers in Thessalonica to think back to the time of his visit and recall their reaction to his preaching. Whatever his opponents might say in his absence, they themselves had responded warmly to his message when he was there in person. Far from viewing it as some concoction of his own, they had come to agree with Paul: he spoke the Word of God. Their reception had been enthusiastic, they had **'welcomed'** it, treating the gospel message as an honoured and well-loved friend. Incidentally, this gives us an insight into Paul's estimate of himself as an apostle of Jesus Christ. His language is reminiscent of the Old Testament prophets who would preface their messages by saying, 'The Word of the Lord came to me,' or 'Thus says the Lord...' It goes a long way to explaining his sheer persistence in the face of massive odds. He was not a self-publicist peddling pet notions of his own. If that had been the case, persecution would have knocked the conceit out of him long before he ever reached Macedonia. He was a spokesman for the Almighty, a herald with the King's message and the King's commission. We often contrast words and actions, as though words are empty, worthless things that compare badly with deeds. On the one hand, some people are 'all talk' while others get things done. The Word of God, however, is a force to be reckoned with: it gets results. When Paul spoke of its effective working in the lives of those who believe, he was reminding the Thessalonian converts that they not only heard what he had said, but had been changed by it.

In this regard, their experience was the same as that of believers elsewhere, particularly in Judea (2:14). Samuel Johnson, the famous literary giant of the eighteenth century, once said, 'I never think I have hit hard unless it rebounds.' In the same way, the antagonism that the early Christians faced was proof of the power of the gospel in their lives. Christianity had made enough of a difference to leave their contemporaries thoroughly rattled. The believers in Thessalonica, who were mostly Gentiles, seem to have been troubled for the most part by their **'own countrymen'**, though these people probably took their cue from the Jews (Acts 17:5). In Judea, however, believers were persecuted by their Jewish neighbours.

Some commentators have argued that Paul's language in verses 15 and 16 betrays a spiteful streak that was unworthy of him. It has even been suggested that he was in a bad mood because of his treatment at the hands of Jews in Corinth. It needs to be said therefore, that there is not a trace of anti-Semitism in the apostle. A Jew himself, with every reason to be proud of his heritage (Phil. 3:4-6), he longed to see the people of his race won to faith in Christ (Rom. 10:1), even saying on one occasion that he would willingly contemplate the loss of his own salvation if that could be the means of bringing it about (Rom. 9:1-5). While his words are far from complimentary, we have to reckon with the fact that they amount to sober reality. Certainly the Jewish race does not bear sole responsibility for the death of Christ. Every human being is implicated to some degree. Even so, it cannot avoid blame altogether. The Jews who bayed for Jesus' execution made a frank admission to Pilate that they had his blood on their hands (Matt. 27:25). Although this is the most heinous case of Jewish rejection of a messenger sent from Jehovah, it is only one of many. Before Jesus came, they persecuted the prophets. Indeed, at this point, Paul does no more than echo the denunciations of his Master (Matt. 23:29-31). The martyr Stephen hinted that not one prophet had avoided persecution (Acts 7:52). In the same way, they continued to maltreat the apostles. In seeking to prevent the spread of the gospel, they were working against the interests of the whole human race. Ultimately, they would only succeed in piling sin upon sin to the point where God would intervene in wrath.

4.
Paul explains his absence from Thessalonica

Please read 1 Thessalonians 2:17 - 3:13

Having cleared himself of the charge that his stay in Thessalonica had been prompted by base motives, Paul went on to answer the accusation that he cared more for his own skin than for his converts and had cleared off, leaving them to face the music. He concluded by stating that he still meant to return when conditions allowed. In this section of his letter, Paul made five points, which taken together leave an impressive body of evidence for the genuineness of his conduct.

His departure from Thessalonica was none of his doing (2:17)

He had been **'taken away'** from his friends. This expression translates a very strong verb. He had been torn from them, wrenched away like an orphan suddenly bereaved of his parents. He wanted them to understand that although his body was elsewhere, his heart remained in Thessalonica.

He had tried to return to Thessalonica (2:17-20)

The phrase **'time and again'** means, at the very least, that Paul had tried more than once to make the journey to Thessalonica in person. In the event, his efforts met with failure. Paul saw the sinister hand of Satan behind this. What form the hindrance took is not mentioned. Various suggestions have been made. Was it the famous 'thorn in the flesh'? (2 Cor. 12:7-10). Whatever this was, Paul himself described it as 'a messenger of Satan'. Perhaps the decision by the rulers of the city, the politarchs, to make Paul's friend Jason stand surety for him was still in effect. Ultimately, we cannot know, but we can take warning that the spiritual warfare that Paul spoke of elsewhere (Eph. 6:10-20) is real. Although his movements are circumscribed by the sovereign purposes of God, Satan has an objective reality and is permitted, in measure, to hamper the servants of God.

At any rate, Paul's repeated attempts to see them in the flesh were a proof of his concern for the Thessalonian believers. The tone of verses 19-20 leaves us in no doubt as to what he thought about them. The **'crown of rejoicing'** is a reference to the crowns won in the games by athletes in the ancient world, the equivalent of a gold medal in the modern Olympics. A rumour was circulating that the Thessalonian Christians meant nothing to Paul. He wanted to make it clear that they meant everything to him!

He had sent Timothy to them (3:1-5)

When it became clear that Paul could not go to Thessalonica in person, he had sent Timothy instead. This had not been an easy decision. On the one hand, the fact that there was no news out of Thessalonica was hard for the apostle to **'endure'**. On the other hand, the thought of being alone in Athens was not pleasant. That city was itself a demanding place for an evangelist, both a hotbed of intellectual activity and a place so steeped in idol-worship (Acts 17:16) that the spiritual atmosphere must have been oppressive. Faced with such a challenge, who would not have preferred Christian companionship to being all alone? Paul saw this as such a daunting prospect that he used a word for **'left'** which was often used to describe what happens when parents die and their children become orphans. It is also clear that Timothy was a person of some calibre. Paul's description of him in verse 2 makes it clear that it would be doubly difficult to part with him. In spite of all this, Paul felt it better to face the challenge of Athens by himself rather than go without some reassurance from Thessalonica.

The purpose behind Timothy's visit was that he might **'establish ... and encourage'** the believers in their faith. Both of these terms are strong. The second carries associations of the way that the Holy Spirit comforts believers, drawing alongside them to stiffen their resolution. All of this was necessary because the faith of the Thessalonian Christians had been tested by various afflictions, particularly the persecution that had come upon them (3:3). Nagging away at Paul's mind was the ugly thought that they might have succumbed to this pressure. This would have invited the conclusion that his efforts had been futile (3:5).

Paul's explanation of his thinking in sending Timothy to Thessalonica also provides us with some helpful instruction on the issue of suffering. Would his friends be **'shaken'** by their experiences? Would they be persuaded to abandon their Christian profession? If they did, life would be a whole lot easier for them. Perhaps, like the followers of Jesus in every period of history, they were tempted to jump to unwarranted conclusions about God himself. Either he does not have the power or the will to prevent the suffering. Either he is not strong enough to shield me from tribulation or he doesn't care! Paul's response is that suffering is part of the purpose of God for his children. It is an inevitable consequence of Christian discipleship (3:3-4).

Nowadays, some believers have been influenced by a strand of teaching which encourages them to believe that God wants all his people to go through life with hardly a flicker of illness, surrounded by material comforts of every kind. The Lord wants his people to travel first class! Christians like that must sooner or later undergo the disillusioning experience of coming face to face with spiritual reality. When trouble comes, in whatever form, they have every right to feel that they have been cheated. No one could level that kind of accusation against Paul. Far from attempting to conceal the cost of discipleship, he had been completely candid about what they could expect once they took up service under the banner of Christ.

Paul's response when Timothy came back (3:6-10)

The genuineness of Paul's concern for the church in Thessalonica was shown by the way that he sent Timothy there when his own precarious situation in Athens would have given him an excuse for hanging on to him. His overjoyed response when Timothy came back (3:6-10) is further evidence that his care ran very deep. The opening phrase **'But now...'** suggests that the apostle could hardly wait to send word back to Thessalonica to say how thrilled he was by all that he had heard. In particular, Timothy's report had quietened his fears that all of his efforts might have been for nothing. Persecution had not succeeded in quenching either their faith in Christ or their love for God and his people. Indeed they still had a place in their hearts for Paul himself. All of this was a weight off his mind: **'Now we live'**! That little phrase speaks volumes. It tells us that a troubled servant of Christ felt able to relax, to breathe again, as it were. Perhaps he also felt that his life was not in vain, that in laying it out for the sake of the gospel he was not spending himself to no purpose.

It is worth noting that Paul's reaction to all this **'good news'** (this, by the way, is the only occasion in the New Testament where this expression is used for anything other than the gospel itself) was to offer thanks to God. There is even a measure of exasperation in his words: 'How can we ever thank God enough?' It would have been so easy for Paul to have taken a different line here. He could, for instance, have congratulated the Thessalonian believers on their staying power. For that matter, he could have congratulated himself: 'See what a great church I've planted!' In fact, the approach adopted in this passage was typical of Paul. It illustrates the fact that he understood the reality of the situation. God had made these believers what they were; the credit was his. Furthermore, there is profound pastoral sense in his approach. To be assured that a mature believer thanks God for us is mightily encouraging without pandering to our tendency to self-promotion.

In passing, it is also worth noting that Paul was encouraged by the spiritual quality of his friends. Christian excellence is a great help to others for it reminds them that the power of God is at work in a human life. Thus it is not only a source of encouragement but a spur and a challenge. It is interesting to see the way that Paul turned his thanks into prayers (3:10). He prayed **'night and day'**, which suggests that he prayed even while he worked with his hands (2:9). He had more than one object in view as he prayed. The opportunity to renew fellowship was obviously one element in his thinking, but even that was subordinated to his great concern to serve them in the cause of the gospel. Not content with the possibility of seeing their faces, he wanted to build them up in their faith by providing teaching that would remedy any deficiencies that were present.

Paul's prayer (3:11-13)

The final evidence that Paul's concern for the church at
Thessalonica was unquestionable comes in the form of a
prayer (3:11-13). It begins with a request that the Lord should
direct his way to them. This in itself is interesting. How natural
it would have been to have written, 'I am hoping to come and
see you'! Paul clearly felt that his movements all took place
under the sovereign control of the Almighty. As the *1689
Confession of Faith* has it, 'Nothing happens by chance or
outside the sphere of God's providence.' His other requests
give us a priceless insight into his priorities. Nothing will show
what really matters to a person so effectively as his or her
prayers. When we pray for others, it will often speak volumes
about our sense of values. For instance, how high a profile do
we give to requests for things that are essentially material —
that a friend will come through an operation or be cured of a
disease, that we ourselves will get the house, job or car that we
have our eyes on? Paul prayed primarily that his friends might
achieve spiritual excellence. He did not see this as the acqui-
sition of some new experience or blessing that they had not
previously enjoyed, but rather that the love that they already
had (3:6) would increase abundantly. Their faith had already
met the test of persecution. Paul was concerned that it should
be so firm that even the events surrounding the return of the
Saviour would not be able to shake them (3:13). The development of mature Christian character would have the opposite
effect. It would vindicate their standing in Christ, establishing
beyond all doubt that they truly were the people of God so that
when Jesus did eventually return with his holy ones, there
would be no doubt that these believers belonged in that exalted
company.

5.
Yield not to temptation!

Please read 1 Thessalonians 4:1-8

The opening words of chapter 4, **'Finally then...'**, encourage us to suppose that Paul is on the point of concluding his epistle, when in actual fact he still has a considerable amount left to say. Nevertheless, we can observe something of a watershed at this point. Paul's subject matter up till now has been largely concerned with his own behaviour, but now his chief objective is to give practical instruction to the Christians in Thessalonica as to how they should behave. It follows that the words 'Finally then...' are not so much an indication that he is about to finish, but rather that a new and important section of the epistle is beginning. It seems likely that Timothy had alerted Paul to a number of problems in the life of the church. We have a clue in 5:14, which suggests that there were three groups of people in the church who were causing concern. Each group faced a tough challenge.

Paul begins by dealing with the *'weak'* (4:3-8). Sexual temptation threatens the Christian at the level of one of the most basic and potent human urges. Would these believers find the strength to resist?

Secondly, Paul concerned himself with the *'unruly'* (4:9-12). This translates a Greek word which was originally used to describe the attitude of an insubordinate soldier, someone who was argumentative and rebellious. By Paul's day it had come to be applied to schoolboys who played truant. The apostle used the term to describe people who were absconding from their work.

Thirdly, Paul addressed himself to the *'faint-hearted'*, an element in the fellowship who were concerned about their departed loved ones (4:13-18) and indeed about their own hopes for salvation (5:1-11).

Sex, work and bereavement figure in the lives of human beings the world over. The modern Christian needs to learn how to live for God in the face of these things every bit as much as the young converts in first-century Thessalonica.

An introductory exhortation (4:1-2)

Paul's language here is very forthright. His concern is that his friends in Macedonia should strive for excellence in their Christian lives. His use of the term **'walk'** includes the idea that believers must not be static. In effect it poses the questions: 'Are we making progress? Are we getting somewhere?' Words like **'urge'** and **'exhort'** make it clear that this is a matter of the highest priority.

This impression is reinforced by the word **'command-ments'**, which translates a word that does not often occur in the New Testament. It is a word with a decidedly military feel to it. It describes orders handed down by those in authority — in this case the highest authority of them all!

Moreover, none of what Paul was about to say would have taken his readers by surprise. He insisted that he was simply reinforcing teaching that they had already **'received'** because he had given it when he was with them in person.

The crux of it all was the principle that they should live so as to **'please God'**. A statement like that has a way of clarifying the issues. Ask how a Christian should live, and it is all too easy to give detailed advice that covers the whole range of life in all its complexity. The heart of it, however, is wonderfully straightforward: whatever the situation, whatever the circumstances, the child of God is to please his Father. This in itself is profoundly challenging. Human nature being what it is, the temptation is to make our own satisfaction our primary goal. Paul urges believers then and now to look beyond their own needs and pleasures and to ask themselves, 'Will the Lord take joy in what I propose to do?'

Paul's advice to the 'weak' (4:3-8)

Verse 3 begins with a general statement. What does please God? The sanctification of his people. Sanctification is not so much a desirable option as something that the Almighty actively desires for each and every believer. This is nothing short of a call for spiritual excellence. The word **'sanctification'** is derived from a Latin word which means 'holy'. To sanctify someone is to make him or her holy. According to the New Testament, this is accomplished in two ways.

First of all, it describes what takes place when God transfers a person from the kingdom of darkness to the kingdom of his Son (Col. 1:13). In that sense, every single believer, however immature, has been sanctified. God has been pleased, in sovereign love, to pluck him out of the broad mass of unsaved humanity and has set him apart for his service. He now belongs to a new category of people. Where once he was a sinner, now he is a saint, one of Jesus' holy people.

Secondly, sanctification also refers to the process whereby the Christian co-operates with the Holy Spirit to grow in Christlikeness. This second meaning is what Paul had in mind when he wrote to his friends in Thessalonica. He wanted them to understand that God actively desires spiritual progress on the part of his people. The same challenge confronts Christians on the verge of the third millennium. We must not allow ourselves to stagnate but must strive to reach new heights of

devotion, new levels of obedience and more consistent usefulness in the service of our Saviour.

Paul wanted to see this at work in a particular area of
Christian character, namely sexual morality. The demands of
real Christianity will often set a person at odds with society.
For first-century believers in a city steeped in the pagan culture
of ancient Greece, the realm of sexual conduct was very much
a case in point. In these verses Paul emphasizes that there is
only one context for the expression of human sexuality, the
union of one man and one woman in a lifelong covenant of
friendship known as marriage. This would have seemed very
strange to first-century Greeks. The idea that a man should
limit himself to his own wife would have seemed puritanical.
What was Paul getting himself excited about? Did he have
something against sex? In any case, it would have been argued,
it is not realistic to expect a man to restrain himself to one
partner. It was more than flesh and blood could stand! Opportunities for extra-marital sex were widely available. It was
accepted that a man did not marry for friendship but to provide
a mother for his legitimate offspring and a manager for his
home. There was no stigma attached to his taking a mistress,
for stimulating companionship as much as for sexual gratification. As for more casual liaisons, the possibilities were
endless. It was not difficult to take advantage of any female
slaves in the household and there were always harlots. Indeed,
prostitution and religion often went hand in hand. Fornication
with prostitutes who were on the staff of many temples was
part and parcel of the ritual demanded by certain cults of the
period. To add to the picture, homosexual relationships were
condoned, even applauded. Over against all this, Paul taught
a high view of marriage. A wife is not a mere domestic skivvy,
nor is she there merely for the purpose of breeding. She is
friend, companion and as such, deserves commitment and
loyalty.

It hardly needs to be said that twentieth-century Britain

bears a striking resemblance to ancient Thessalonica. The Christian is called to live by the biblical ideal in a climate where sexual experimentation before marriage is regarded as a legitimate leisure activity for teenagers and where extra-marital affairs, instead of being condemned outright as the betrayal of a sacred promise, are regarded as a permissible outlet for those trapped in an unfulfilling marriage. The aggressive and self-confident 'gay' lobby has almost succeeded in gaining a measure of public acceptance for its case that stable homosexual relationships should have equal status with conventional heterosexual marriages.

Once again, it must be insisted that the only God-given context for sexual activity is marriage. It follows that heterosexual liaisons before marriage (fornication), or outside of it (adultery) and any kind of homosexual union are forbidden. Each man, says Paul, should confine himself to his own wife (4:4). Some commentators have argued that the word translated **'vessel'** refers not to a man's wife but to his own body. The argument is essentially that to compare a wife to a vessel is uncomplimentary. If this is what Paul had in mind, we still have the necessary point that sexual immorality is in part a sin against one's own body. Even so, 'wife' seems the most likely rendering of the disputed word for the following reasons:

1. The word translated **'possess'** actually means to acquire or take. A man may acquire a wife, but has a body from the outset.

2. The word 'vessel' is used as a metaphor for human beings in the New Testament. We are the 'earthen vessels' which contain the treasure of God's grace (2 Cor. 4:7). In one place it is even used of wives, who are described as 'weaker vessels' (1 Peter 3:7). Incidentally, this does not mean that one sex is strong and the other weak, but that in certain respects, one is weak and the other is weaker.

3. Since Paul is making a stern case against adultery and fornication, the natural way to read this passsage is that he is not so much saying that these are sins against one's own body, but contrasting them with marriage. Within the married relationship, sexual relations are holy and honourable. Outside it, they are sinful and shameful (4:4).

4. Paul's argument here anticipates a fuller statement of the same principle in 1 Corinthians 7:2-9: 'Nevertheless, because of sexual immorality, let each man have his own wife, and let each woman have her own husband. Let the husband render to his wife the affection due her, and likewise also the wife to her husband. The wife does not have authority over her own body, but the husband does. And likewise the husband does not have authority over his own body, but the wife does. Do not deprive one another except with consent for a time, that you may give yourselves to fasting and prayer; and come together again, so that Satan does not tempt you because of your lack of self-control. But I say this as a concession, not as a commandment. For I wish that all men were even as I myself. But each one has his own gift from God, one in this manner, and another in that. But I say to the unmarried and to the widows: It is good for them if they remain even as I am; but if they cannot exercise self-control, let them marry. For it is better to marry than to burn.'

Paul's teaching also has something to say about the nature of sexual conduct within marriage. The married relationship is not a legalized sexual free-for-all. **'Honour'** is contrasted with **'the passion of lust'** (4:4,5). A wife or a husband is more than a tool for sexual gratification. The tabloid newspapers speak of 'sexploitation'. It is a sad fact this takes place in the homes of married couples. It is a chilling matter to realize that police estimate that the overwhelming majority of rapes are domestic. The expression of sexual love, as of any other kind of love, should be guided by the kind of demeanour portrayed for us in 1 Corinthians 13.

There is more to adultery than mere sex. Paul's use of terms like **'take advantage'** and **'defraud'** (4:6) remind us that such considerations as the betrayal of one's own partner and the theft of another's come into play. In one sense, sex is almost incidental. Adultery is primarily about broken promises and ruthless self-assertion. An adulterer is a cheat. If only more people would reckon with the fact that the Lord will settle scores in due course! No one gets away with it, even if society at large has ceased to condemn. The Lord who sees everything is aware of what goes on in the nation's bedrooms. To sum up, we are to glorify God in our sex lives, both in the things we refrain from doing and the things that we do. Paul does not insist here on an antiquated set of cultural norms, but the will of God himself (4:7-8). The Spirit of God who has taken up residence in the Christian is holy. An undisciplined sex life is one way of grieving him.

It is worth recognizing that single believers can face a particularly acute challenge in this area. They have no legitimate outlet whatever for what can be a very insistent appetite. They need the prayers of Christian friends. Nevertheless it is important that they recognize, as John Stott says, that 'We shall not become a bundle of frustrations and inhibitions if we embrace God's standard, but only if we rebel against it. Christ's yoke is easy, provided that we submit to it. It is possible for human sexual energy to be redirected ... both into affectionate relationships with friends of both sexes and into the loving service of others. Multitudes of Christian singles, both men and women, can testify to this. Alongside a natural loneliness, accompanied sometimes by acute pain, we can find joyful self-fulfilment in the self-giving service of God and other people.'

6.
The Christian's attitude to work

Please read 1 Thessalonians 4:9-12

We have seen that there were three groups of people in the church at Thessalonica who were causing concern. Having dealt with those 'weak' individuals who seemed as though their resistance might crumple in the face of sexual temptation, Paul turns his attention to another group whom he describes as the 'unruly'. This element in the church posed a considerable pastoral challenge. Their conduct was such that they needed a stiff warning (5:14). It is difficult, at this distance, to be certain about the conduct of this group. The passage contains two helpful clues, however. First of all, as we saw in the previous chapter, the word translated 'unruly' was sometimes used to describe schoolboys who played truant. Secondly, the fact that Paul sees the antidote to unruly behaviour as being honest toil suggests that these people were absconding from their work.

Among the ancient Greeks, work was often regarded as demeaning: that was what slaves were for! As soon as a person's finances allowed, the done thing was to hire domestic labour so that he could be freed for the pursuits of the intellect and the demands of leisure and society. Perhaps some of the Christians in Thessalonica were still trapped by this kind of mind-set.

Over against this, there is also the possibility that some had reacted irresponsibly to the widespread excitement about the return of Jesus Christ by giving up work on the grounds that there was no need for it if the Saviour could return at any moment.

Paul's advice to the 'unruly' (4:9-12)

It should not surprise us that Paul begins with a general statement about **'brotherly love'** (4:9-10). The believers in Thessalonica were already good examples of the kind of mutual love that should characterize all Christians. Not only did they exhibit this love among themselves, it also spilled over to the wider circle of Christians in the whole province of Macedonia. Paul's concern was simply that his readers should build on this excellent beginning by showing the same love **'more and more'**.

This opening was necessary because a right attitude to work will stem from an awareness of the claims of love. Conscientious work would produce a situation where the believers would **'lack nothing'** (4:12). In effect, Paul was urging the point that independence, while it can be overdone, indicates that we love our neighbours. If we turn this on its head it soon becomes clear: love does not sponge on others! This explains his command in verse 11 that all the Christians in Thessalonica should aspire to be productive members of society who paid their own way in the world by working hard. The person who refuses to work when work is available cannot excuse his laziness on the grounds that he is so preoccupied with spiritual things that it would be wrong to descend from his exalted plane to the lowly world of mere physical toil. People like that expect to be fed and clothed through the efforts of others. They exploit the good will of those whom they affect to despise for not giving themselves up to the pursuit of higher things! But love does not take advantage of the generosity of others.

In addition to this, the apostle had in mind the fact that the Christian is always being watched by the world at large (4:12). 'The fear of man brings a snare' (Prov. 29:25), but it is also wise to remember that our behaviour has an effect on other people and that laziness brings disrepute on the gospel. This is Paul's reason for what may seem a contradictory piece of advice. Ambition so often goes hand in hand with a desire for prominence and public acclaim. The Christian, however, must make it his ambition not to attract attention for anything other than dependability and hard graft.

7.
Paul's advice to the faint-hearted

Please read 1 Thessalonians 4:13 - 5:11

Having dealt with the problems posed by the 'weak' and the 'unruly', Paul addresses himself in the third place to the 'faint-hearted', an element in the fellowship who were concerned about their departed loved ones (4:13-18) and indeed about their own hopes for salvation (5:1-11). This section provides us with instruction about two of the issues that are involved in the wider subject of 'eschatology', the Bible's teaching about the last things, both as they affect individual people and the human race at large. This, of course, cannot be separated from the event which will form the climax of human history, the return of Jesus Christ to this earth.

It is important that we grasp Paul's purpose in writing as he did. It was not his intention to provide an exhaustive account of all that will take place at the end. Nothing is said here, for instance, about the resurrection of unbelievers. The apostle confines himself to answering questions which had evidently arisen in the minds of his friends in Thessalonica and which were, no doubt, relayed to him by Timothy. The first concerned the fate of those Christians who had already died (4:13-18) and the second, the timing of the end (5:1-11).

Comfort for the bereaved (4:13-18)

Paul's argument in these verses suggests that a number of
believers from the church in Thessalonica had died since he
himself had been there. Their grieving relatives and friends
appear to have been worried that since their loved ones had
died prior to Jesus' return, they would somehow be at a
disadvantage compared with those who **'are alive and remain'** (4:15). We are not told exactly what it was that troubled
the bereaved, but at the very least they seem to have been
gripped by anxiety in case those whom they mourned should
miss out because they would not be around at the time when
the Saviour came back. Had they perhaps jumped to the
conclusion that salvation depended on being alive at that time?
Whatever the precise nature of their problem, the apostle was
at pains to reassure them that their departed loved ones would
be none the worse for having gone before.

It is worth noting here that Paul refers to the believing dead
as **'those who sleep'** (4:13,14,15). It is not surprising that
many cultures refer to death as a kind of sleep. The word
'cemetery' is derived from a Greek word that means 'place of
sleep'. The stillness of a corpse bears a certain resemblance to
a person in slumber. Furthermore, it is a phrase which occurs
from time to time in the Old Testament, where we read that this
or that monarch 'slept with his fathers'. The main idea in such
cases seems to have been that these figures were now at rest
after a lifetime of strenuous activity. 'Sleep' is a word that
promises a great deal; it reminds us that physical death is not
the end. Those who go to bed at night expect to get up in the
morning! Viewed from that perspective, cemeteries are mere
dormitories. When the great alarm sounds, those who inhabit
them will rise from their slumber. Death loses much of its
power to terrify us when we can begin to think of it in these
terms. What could be more homely than calmly settling

oneself down to sleep in full confidence that morning, when it comes, will bring a new and better life altogether?

Some believers have concluded from this that the dead are not conscious, that the soul is at rest as well as the body and will remain so until Jesus comes once more. Over against this, the Bible affirms that while the body sleeps, the soul goes immediately to its reward to be reunited with a glorified body when the believing dead are raised to life. As he suffered on the cross, Jesus promised that the repentant thief would be with him in paradise that very day (Luke 23:43). It seems rather forced to suggest that it would not actually be 'today', but would merely feel like it because he would spend the intervening centuries in a kind of coma. Paul echoed the teaching of his Master. He once confessed to being well pleased with the prospect of being 'absent from the body' for this would mean that he was 'present with the Lord' (2 Cor. 5:8). Why should this thought please him if he could not enjoy the Lord's presence because he did not expect to be conscious of it? Are we to read those majestic words, 'For to me, to live is Christ, and to die is gain' (Phil. 1:21) to mean, 'I will be much better off when I die, but wholly unaware of the fact'? The Christian hope, while it is not fully realized until the Second Coming, is not deferred until then. Like the Thessalonians, we may comfort ourselves concerning our departed brothers and sisters with the assurance that they are supremely happy in the presence of Jesus.

Paul opened his treatment of this subject by saying that he wanted his teaching to have an effect on their conduct (4:13). Once they understood the true situation as it affected their deceased brothers and sisters they would not be prone to the same desperate grieving as their pagan neighbours. This is not to say that Christians do not grieve at all. John's account of the only sinless man shedding tears beside the tomb of his friend Lazarus (John 11:35) is a pointed reminder that it is not wrong as such to mourn someone who was dear to us and who has been taken from us. The difference, however, between the Christian and the **'others'** is that he grieves over a temporary separation. When one believer looks at the coffin of another, there is no cause to give way to that heart-wrenching cry: 'I'm never going to see him again!'

Paul went on to make a strong affirmation of the truths which lie at the heart of the Christian faith (4:14). The object of our faith is a crucified and risen Saviour who will certainly return to the world that he left at the time of his resurrection. This will not be a solitary return; he will be escorted by an enormous multitude, for he **'will bring with him those who sleep in Jesus'**. After all, those believers who have died during the long interval between Jesus' life on earth and the present time have left their bodies behind and are 'present with the Lord'. Paul anticipated an occasion of awesome splendour, a display of overwhelming force intended to cow the powers of darkness into submission, a victory parade. 'Behold, the Lord comes with ten thousands of his saints' (Jude 1:14). Even the most determined opponent of the gospel will quail at such a sight, but the believer will find it the most welcome event he has ever witnessed, for it will be the long-awaited homecoming of his Saviour, accompanied by a great host of believing friends who have gone before.

It is worth noting that the one who is to come, bringing his people with him, is **'God'**. We are not merely to expect a visit from an archangel, but from the most exalted personage of all. The King of the universe is coming in royal pomp to hold his rebel dominions to account and to reward his loyal subjects.

In particular, this all means that the fears of the Thessalonian Christians concerning their departed loved ones were groundless (4:15). Those believers who are alive when the last day of all breaks for this sad world will not experience blessings that will be denied those who have gone before.

The sequence of events (4:16-17)

In order to clarify the picture still further, the apostle provided his friends in Thessalonica with an outline of the events of the final day of our planet's history (16,17). The sequence is as follows:

1. **'The Lord himself will descend from heaven.'** It is often stressed that our Saviour's return will be visible: 'Behold, he is coming with clouds, and every eye will see him' (Rev. 1:7). It also needs to be said that it will be audible. Peter speaks of the destruction of the heavens and earth that exist at present being announced by 'a great noise' (2 Peter 3:10). Paul is even more specific. There has been some debate about the **'shout'**, the **'voice of an archangel'** and the **'trumpet of God'**. Are these to be three distinct noises? I prefer the view that they are different ways of describing one colossal eruption of sound which will impinge on the consciousness of every human soul, both the living and the dead. No one will sleep through it!

The 'shout' recalls the great word of power which brought Lazarus of Bethany out of the tomb, even though he had been dead for four days and was in an advanced state of putrefaction (John 11:43). It also reminds us that the same Jesus who summoned his friend from the regions of the dead has promised that at the appointed time, 'All who are in the graves will hear his voice and come forth', some to 'the resurrection of life' and others to 'the resurrection of condemnation' (John 5:28-29). The one spoken summons will have a radically different effect on those who hear it. To some it will be a call to rise to an eternity of joy; to others it will be the prelude to their being despatched to endless loss and misery. Those believers in Thessalonica who had been anxious about their brothers and sisters in Christ who had already died would understand this to mean that their departed friends would hear a joyful summons to enter the blessedness of their Lord.

The 'voice of an archangel' is itself a reminder of the dramatic picture painted by the apostle John where a mighty angel announces the conclusion of God's purposes: 'There should be delay no longer'! (Rev. 10:6). The clear, piercing note of the trumpet also points us back to the Old Testament. On the one hand, it recalls those occasions during the Israelites' long journey through the deserts of Sinai when the sound of a trumpet was a summons to approach the tabernacle. This was a sombre affair, a call for sinners to draw near the one who is holy. On the other hand, we must not forget that once the Israelites were settled in the promised land, the year of Jubilee was announced with a trumpet blast (Lev. 25:8-17). This was a very welcome sound indeed, for it meant the cancellation of all debts! In the same way, the cataclysmic sound which will herald the close of this present age will fill the hearts of some with terror, while those who belong to Christ will be thrilled to hear it.

2. Before anything else happens, **'The dead in Christ will rise first'** (4:16). It would appear that at this point the saints who have accompanied the Lord on his triumphal return are reunited with their bodies, now risen and glorified.

3. Next, those saints who have not tasted death will be **'caught up'** to **'meet the Lord in the air'**, together with those who have. The phrase 'caught up' translates a term which is very dramatic. It means to be firmly plucked up from our present position and placed elsewhere. This

event has often been called the 'rapture'. That is because
the word 'rapture', which nowadays usually describes a
state of unusual emotional intensity, once meant that a
person had been forcibly seized (it comes from the same
Latin root as the word 'rape'). When I was a young
Christian, the word 'rapture' was often prefaced by the
word 'secret'. It was argued that the Lord would come
'for his saints' without revealing himself to mankind at
large, that some time would elapse (usually seven years)
and then he would come 'with his saints'. The first of
these comings would be marked by the removal of all
believers from this earth. To the human race at large, it
would seem that the troublesome Christians had all
simultaneously disappeared without trace. Preachers
liked to ram the point home by describing the aeroplane
with an unbelieving co-pilot who suddenly found himself in charge of the aircraft because the born-again pilot
was no longer at his side. This view requires us to believe
that there will, in effect, be two second comings, the first
of which is neither audible nor visible and the second of
which is both! I can see that a rapture is taught in these
verses, but there is no support for the idea that it will be
secret. The trumpet call and the appearance of the Lord
of glory will make it the most public event in the history
of this globe.

The purpose of the 'rapture' is that we might 'meet
the Lord'. The word 'meet' is a technical term. Theologians often refer to the Second Coming of Jesus as his
'parousia'. This was a word which described the visit
made to a particular city by an important dignitary,
perhaps even the reigning monarch. While the eminent
personage was still on his way to the favoured city, the
citizens would go out to 'meet' him and then accompany
him on the remainder of his journey. This helps us to

complete our picture of the events of the tremendous day which will bring all things to their appointed conclusion. In particular, it helps us to see that the events of that day will be a unified whole. The King of kings will have an escort of overjoyed people from among the inhabitants of this planet. They will comprise two contingents. The souls of the believing dead, now reunited with their bodies, will rise to meet the Sovereign of the skies, while those believers who are alive will also form part of the throng who go out in joy to join the train of the approaching monarch. Not all will have 'slept', but all will have been 'changed' (1 Cor. 15:51-54), for the word of command which neither the living nor the dead can resist is the word of power that finally clothes what was once mortal with immortality.

5. Then comes the grand reunion. The word **'together'** is particularly important. It reminds us that the conclusion of these tremendous events will be the most thrilling reunion that ever took place. Separation will be a thing of the past.

First of all, every believer, all those who have died in years gone by as well as those who are alive at the time, will be united with his Lord. In the here and now, what we know of the presence of Christ is ministered to us by the Holy Spirit through the means that God has appointed. When the great day dawns, however, the longed-for moment will have arrived. Every Christian will look upon the face of Jesus! And this will be no brief treat. We shall not be required, after a period of time, to go back to the present situation where we meet our beloved in prayer, Bible-reading and the ordinances of the local church. We shall enjoy face-to-face contact with the Lover of our souls for ever. It is a prospect which sets the pulse racing. The years that must pass before it

all breaks in upon us will seem like seconds once the joy
of it has burst upon us.

Secondly, we shall be together with our brothers and
sisters — the whole family reunited at last.

This is why Paul concludes as he does with an exhortation
to the Christians in Thessalonica (4:18). No one is exempt
from the pain of separation. Partings are a continual feature of
life in this world. They may be acrimonious: friends quarrel
and do not always make it up. Sometimes they are barely
perceptible. Months or even years pass before we realize that
we have drifted apart from someone whose friendship once
mattered very much indeed. Often partings are temporary: the
teenage son returns to his mother when the college term is
over. Death, however, twists the knife in the wound. At least
in this life, it causes a rupture that cannot be mended. Once a
person has died there is no possibility for his estranged friends
to seek reconciliation, his wife may lament all the occasions
that she failed to tell him that she loved him, and then there is
the sickening realization that he has not gone on holiday only
to return in a fortnight. The dead do not return. Even the
Christian life has a bittersweet quality, for the Lord who loves
us so well and whom we love so feebly is at a remove from us.
For the unbeliever, this is a situation that will never be put
right. Separated from God in the here and now because of his
wilfulness and sin, he will have to endure that separation for
ever. In the face of death we can offer no comfort whatever to
such a person. Believers, however, can encourage each other.
Not for the Christian the bleakness of the grave and the empti-
ness of eternal ruin. Paul would have us spur one another on.
Jesus is coming! Many dear friends are coming with him. Soon
partings will be abolished, undertakers will all be redundant,
for the Lord and his people will all be together, never to be
separated.

Counsel about the end (5:1-11)

Why did Paul raise this matter of **'the times and the seasons'**? (5:1). His friends in Thessalonica were clearly deeply preoccupied with the whole question. When would the **'day of the Lord'** (5:2) come? Two areas of concern might have prompted their curiosity.

In the first place, we know that there was some anxiety about believers from Thessalonica who had already died. Would this place them at a disadvantage when the Lord returned? In the same way, some of the believers might have been worried about themselves. If they happened to die prior to the coming of Christ, would they, like those who had already gone before, miss out in some way on the blessings of the world to come? For people who were troubled in this way, it would matter a great deal if they could have some estimate as to the date of the end. The nearer it was, the less likelihood there would be that they would be cheated by death! If indeed there were Christians in Thessalonica who thought that way, they need fear no longer. Paul's teaching that those who 'are alive and remain' will not benefit from 'the coming of the Lord' (4:15) in ways that are denied to those who sleep should have quietened all their anxieties.

Secondly, there may well have been others who felt that a knowledge of the precise timescale for the last things is an indispensable aid to preparation for the events themselves. A deadline often helps to clarify the mind. When a student knows the date of his finals he can devote himself to revision. Time is short; he must get down to it. Similarly, once a young couple preparing for marriage have set the date for their wedding, they have a powerful incentive to sort out all the necessary arrangements. A venue must be booked for the reception, a photographer hired, bridesmaids' dresses ordered and all the rest of the paraphernalia seen to. Our day-to-day lives easily become cluttered. A deadline forces us to settle on our priorities and pursue them ruthlessly.

1. The Lord will return suddenly, like a 'thief in the night'

Paul's response was to remind his friends of something that they ought to have remembered. It is highly unlikely that anyone will ever succeed in making an accurate prediction about the timing of the end, the final entry as it were, in the personal organizer. All we can say with any safety is that it is now much closer than it was when Paul wrote these words. Date-setting is a pointless exercise. That is because the **'day of the Lord so comes as a thief in the night'** (5:2). This idea, that the returning Saviour will come without warning, like a burglar, originates with Jesus himself (Matt. 24:43). It is also used elsewhere in the New Testament (2 Peter 3:10; Rev. 3:3; 16:15). It is intended to teach us that this is an event which will catch a great many people unawares.

It follows that for the vast majority of people alive at the time, our Saviour's return will be completely unexpected. It will have all the suddenness of a lightning bolt out of a clear sky. The futurologists who subscribe to the theory that we will gradually pollute ourselves to death assume that there will be a period of some decades when we will be able to see the end slowly advancing to meet us. There are even Christian pundits who argue that a whole series of calamitous events will happen in a given order and lend an element of predictability to it all. Put that kind of thinking out of your mind! A friend or relative who means to pay a visit may well write or telephone in advance to make sure that he doesn't arrive only to find an empty house, but no burglar who means to make a success of his trade announces his visits.

In order to ram this point home, the Lord Jesus once said that the end would resemble the world as it was in 'the days of

Noah' (see Matt. 24:36-39). The day appointed for the close of human history will dawn like any other day. Normality will be the keynote. The human race will go about its collective business as it always has done. From the perspective of most people, the end will come when they least expect it.

This is borne out in verse 3, where Paul pictures the world at the time of the end. Contentment reigns! Throughout the world, the dominant assessment of the situation is **'Peace and safety!'** — all's well! This only means that mankind at large has entertained a false sense of security. Our English translations do not quite capture the dramatic nature of Paul's word-order: **'Then a sudden thing comes: destruction!'** The last thing that unbelievers anticipated has come upon them.

It is worth pausing for a moment to consider the thrust of that word 'destruction'. It is sometimes used as ammunition by those who argue against the doctrine of eternal punishment, the Bible's teaching that those who die without God's forgiveness can expect an eternity of endless and conscious torment. The suggestion has been put forward that God punishes people in a way that has eternal consequences, but not that he inflicts a punishment which they experience for eternity. The argument is that 'destruction' means that the person in question is annihilated, he ceases to be. Certainly in everyday English, when we destroy a thing it is no longer there. Paul, however, had something else in mind, namely that the person who is destroyed continues to exist but is damaged beyond repair. He does not become a non-person, but the wreck of a human being. When God pours out his wrath on unrepentant sinners, they will not be annihilated so much as ruined.

2. The Lord's return will be inexorable, like the birth pangs of a woman in labour

The apostle also has a second illustration for us, that of the pregnant woman. In one sense, the onset of labour pains is not a sudden thing in the way that a visit from a burglar might be. It is not altogether unexpected. As soon as the woman in question realizes that she is expecting a child, she must reckon with the fact that she can have some idea, to within a month or so, of the likely time of delivery. Paul's concern at this point, however, was to show that the day of the Lord is inevitable. Once the mother-to-be starts to experience the contractions that mark the onset of labour, she can be sure that a process is under way which cannot be reversed. Things must take their course. In the same way, once the end of all things is upon us, it will be too late for those who are not prepared to escape the inevitable outcome.

3. Be prepared!

How can we prepare for the end? Paul addresses this matter in 1 Thessalonians 5:4-8. In essence, his message is that our reaction to the final cataclysm will depend entirely upon our attitude. Most people, says Paul, are unprepared. They are caught out by the stealthy burglar because they are in the dark, asleep or drunk. These are different ways of describing the plight of the person who is not alive to God. Darkness is an effective way of describing his state of mind. As far as spiritual reality is concerned, he cannot see clearly. In the same way, he is unresponsive to the promptings of God, like a man in a deep sleep who cannot be roused. He also resembles the drunk because his mind is befuddled. Just as the person who is intoxicated cannot relate to his surroundings, a person who does not know God is incapable of responding to the overtures of grace.

This state of mind is not universal. Paul did not suppose, for instance, that it characterized his friends in Thessalonica. It was the 'others' who were so afflicted. It is a common idea in Scripture that the human race is divided into two categories, variously described as the saved and the lost, the sheep and the goats, the children of God and the offspring of Satan. Here the same thought is expressed with reference to those who are the **'sons of light'** (5:5). These are contrasted with those who are **'of the darkness'**. Calling someone a 'son of' a particular thing is a typically Hebrew way of observing that it is his predominant characteristic. Either we belong to the light or the darkness. Our whole nature will be shot through with the one or the other. In particular, those who have been touched by the light will not be taken by surprise when the end comes. They will be expecting it, ready for it, because they have learned to live in a perpetual state of watchfulness.

In brief, Paul urged the members of the church in Thessalonica to prepare for the coming day of the Lord, not by trying to fix the date, but by putting themselves on the alert. This explains his portrait of the soldier in verse 8. The Christian is like a man on sentry duty. It is his responsibility to keep himself awake and on the lookout. The idea of a soldier equipped for battle is one that Paul used a number of times. In each case, he felt free to vary the detail of the soldier's equipment according to whichever point he wished to make. Here the armour is purely defensive: the head and the trunk are covered. The essential point is that he is protected against surprise concerning the coming of Christ and the end of this present scheme of things. Faith, love and hope are the three great Christian virtues. Like the soldier in his bullet-proof vest who is able to resist the shock of a sniper's bullet when it comes from an unexpected quarter, the person who possesses faith, hope and love is armed and ready to face a future which will destroy those who do not share this vital equipment.

All along, in speaking of the **'day of the Lord'**, Paul was quite deliberately using a phrase which first occurs in the Old Testament. It is impossible to read it here without a deep sense of foreboding. Consider this warning from the prophet Amos:

> Woe to you who desire the day of the Lord!
> For what good is the day of the Lord to you?
> It will be darkness, and not light.
> It will be as though a man fled from a lion,
> And a bear met him;
> Or as though he went into the house,
> Leaned his hand on the wall,
> And a serpent bit him.
> Is not the day of the Lord darkness, and not light?
> Is it not very dark, with no brightness in it?
>
> (Amos 5:18-20).

In the same way, the apostle Peter speaks of a day when 'The elements will melt with fervent heat' (2 Peter 3:10-13) and the fabric of the created universe will be dissolved.

'**Wrath**', however, is not what the Christian anticipates (5:9). The thunderclap that announces judgement on those who have defied God also proclaims the long-awaited day of salvation. A day of unbridled terror for the unbeliever will, at one and the same time, be a day of boundless joy for those who know that it spells the completion of their deliverance from sin and the imminence of their never-ceasing union with the God they love.

It is worth noting Paul's use of the word '**appoint**'. It reminds us that our salvation originates in God himself. While we are called upon to repent and to entrust ourselves and our future to the mercy of Christ, the very repentance that we practise and the faith that we exercise are not merely acts of the new nature but the gifts of a generous God (Acts 5:31; Eph. 2:8). It is impossible to speak of salvation without speaking of Jesus Christ. Pardon for sin is only available because he has died in the place of sinners.

This section of the letter closes with a challenge that all the believers in Thessalonica should take responsibility for one another (5:11). If the present seemed threatening, the future could not be brighter. Paul was aware that his friends already appreciated how important it was to strengthen those who were feeling discouraged. Let them go on from this good beginning; let each of them excel in the business of fortifying and building up his or her brothers and sisters. Modern Christians who respond to Paul's challenge can be sure that they are doing something to meet a real need. I am often left with the impression that the present generation of the Lord's people are not buoyed up with hope because they are gripped by the prospect of Christ's return. An injection of confidence is a vital necessity. Who will take it upon themselves to provide it?

8.
What it means to be a local church

Please read 1 Thessalonians 5:12-22

As we examine the concluding section of this epistle, it would be tempting to make the mistaken assumption that this is nothing more than a tailpiece which contains a series of exhortations plucked out of the air at random. The unifying idea in these verses is that the Thessalonian Christians should learn increasingly what it means to be a church, a local expression of the body of Christ. This explains Paul's repetition of the word **'brethren'** (5:12,14,25,26,27). His emphasis is as valid now as then. If a particular fellowship of believers is to function as it should, each and every member has a part to play. It is a fatal error to suppose that the appointment of a minister absolves the membership at large of any responsibility for the success or failure of that fellowship to be the kind of church that the Lord would have it be. With this in mind, Paul examines three areas of local church life, namely the attitude of members towards the church leadership (5:12-13), to one another (5:14-15) and towards their corporate worship (5:16-28).

The local church and its leaders (5:12-13)

When Paul planted churches, he saw to it that suitably qualified men were ordained as elders in each congregation (Acts

14:23). This was evidently the case in Thessalonica. Perhaps
the two men who are mentioned by name, Aristarchus and
Secundus (Acts 20:4; 27:2), were among them. At any rate,
there seems to have been a measure of tension within the
church. Why did Paul feel it necessary to encourage the
brothers and sisters to **'recognize'**, or appreciate those who
were their leaders? Presumably because, among the other
things that he had mentioned, Timothy had reported that the
opposite was taking place. The oversight of the church had
come in for criticism. How had this arisen? We do know that
one element in the congregation was 'unruly' (5:14). A segment of the fellowship had developed the irresponsible habit
of absenting themselves from work. We cannot be certain, but
it seems possible that the elders of the church had already
attempted to deal with these people, who responded by making
their resentment plain. At this distance, we cannot tell whether
the church leadership had been unduly heavy-handed, or
whether the problem lay solely with the hurt pride of the
members in question.

The relationship between church members and those who
occupy positions of spiritual leadership is a subject that has
attracted a great deal of attention in the recent past. First of all,
at least in the Free Church tradition, there has been a reaction
against the perceived clericalism of the ministerial caste. The
recovery of the principle that leadership should be the shared
responsibility of a body of elders has been an overdue correc-
tive to the problems which have arisen when authority has
been concentrated in the hands of a single individual. 'One-
man ministry' will no longer do! Similarly, it has helped to
correct the assumption that the paid minister is the only person
in the gathering who can exercise certain kinds of ministry.
The idea that ministers ought to be competent in every area of
Christian service has produced an enormous number of casu-
alties down the years as men have been crushed by the weight
of unrealistic expectations.

Alongside this development, attempts have also been made to recover biblical church discipline. This has sparked off considerable debate, because in some circles the pendulum has swung to the opposite extreme. It is not difficult to find examples of leaders who have no standards and will tolerate anything, nor is it hard to find others who throw their weight about. How are we to establish the scriptural happy medium between laxity and heavy-shepherding?

The qualities of elders

Paul makes three observations which, taken together, give us a portrait of spiritual leadership at its best:

1. *Good elders work hard.* They **'labour'** among their brothers and sisters. This is a word normally associated with arduous physical toil. In today's world, many suppose that those in the paid ministry have an easy time of it: a full week's pay for a single day's work! In actual fact, the task of a minister unites a number of different aspects, each of which is very demanding. The preparation and the delivery of sermons, the work that consistent intercession naturally involves and the emotionally draining business of providing spiritual counsel can all sap the strength of someone with a robust constitution. And what of those elders who work at other occupations and therefore care for the churches in what is laughably called their 'spare time'? Nevertheless, the people of God have a right to expect that those whom they entrust with positions of authority work diligently, as Paul himself did (2:9). The challenge to church members is to ask themselves, when they are blessed with such conscientious leaders, whether or not they appreciate their efforts.

2. *Good elders have authority.* They **'over'** the people of God. This introduces a subject which requires a delicate

balance. On the one hand, leadership in the Christian community is to be distinctly different from the approach that is often
apparent in the world at large. The apostle Peter emphasized
that elders are not to behave as 'lords' over those in their care
(1 Peter 5:3). This echoes the example of the Lord Jesus who
often made the point that his behaviour was a marked contrast
to that of the 'rulers of the Gentiles'. He told his disciples that
'Whoever desires to become great among you, let him be your
servant. And whoever desires to be first among you, let him be
your slave...' He himself gave a potent demonstration of this
principle in action by giving his life 'as a ransom for many'
(Matt. 20:25-28). His verdict on his life was: 'I am among you
as the one who serves' (Luke 22:27). In short, the elders who
oversee local churches have no justification for behaving like
Protestant mini-popes, or adopting the 'Rambo' style of much
secular management which insists on the 'right to manage',
often to the detriment of its workforce. It is to be the humble
leadership of the servant!

On the other hand, however, this does not mean that elders
are to become doormats. A genuine measure of authority is
part and parcel of the office.

Perhaps the best way of grasping the biblical style of leadership is by considering the description of the elder in 1 Timothy
3:1-7, where 'rule' over the church is compared with 'rule'
over a family. The authority of elders, then, is that of the concerned parent.

3. Good elders are not spineless. They have a duty to **'admonish'** those who require it. This term translates a strong Greek
word which refers to the kind of emphatic warning that might
be given to someone who is on the point of 'going off the rails'.
Certainly Paul himself did not shirk from pointing out the
consequences of foolish and sinful behaviour to his friends in
the churches at Ephesus (Acts 20:31) and Corinth (1 Cor.

4:14). Ultimately, elders may have to confront the fact that those who do not heed such warnings may well become liable to church discipline. Incidentally, 'admonish' is such a strong word, with a pronounced negative emphasis, that it is often used in tandem with teaching (Col 1:28; 3:16).

The response of the membership

Given that the elders are all that they should be, how should the members of the local church conduct themselves towards them? Paul makes three further observations:

1. Good elders deserve recognition. On the one hand, they are not to be flattered and treated like royalty, while on the other, they are not be treated with contempt as though they could be hired and fired at will. The dismissal of one minister of the gospel prompted the observation that independent evangelical ministers in England have as much security as pianists who perform in public houses!

2. Good elders deserve affection as well as appreciation. Paul argues here that the demanding nature of their work should evoke a high level of genuine love and gratitude. Some ministers have left one church for another, only to find that the members of the first church were genuinely sorry to see them go and reacted to their impending departure as though it amounted to a bereavement. What made this experience disconcerting was that during all the years of a long pastorate there had been little indication that their feelings ran so deep.

3. Good elders deserve loyalty. Nothing holds the work of a local church back more than internal strife, which is why Paul insists that the believers in Thessalonica should be at peace among themselves (5:13). In particular, this means that wrangling between elders and members must cease. How many churches are bedevilled by destructive tensions between the leaders and the led? It is right to insist that leaders do not ride roughshod over the sensitivities of the church members and equally right to insist that the latter do not thwart the plans of the elders with belligerent obstructionism.

The local church fellowship (5:14-15)

We have considered Paul's teaching on spiritual leadership in verses 12 and 13. Now in verses 14 and 15 the apostle introduces another dimension of church life, the mutual care that members ought to have for one another. There is a connection here with what has gone before. Who should shoulder the burden of warning the unruly, comforting the faint-hearted and upholding the weak? Ask this question of many a church member and the answer would be: the pastor, or perhaps the elders. As far as Paul was concerned, these vital pastoral tasks were not the sole province of the top tier of church leadership. One certain way of ensuring that the job is done badly is to leave it to the oversight. There is simply too much to be done! That is why Paul emphasized that these tasks were the responsibility of the membership at large.

The congregation at Thessalonica included people who were a source of concern for a variety of reasons. Some were **'unruly'**. These believers had become so besotted with the thought of Christ's return that they had given up going to work. Such conduct brought the gospel into disrepute. Honest toil is a moral duty, which when carried out in the right spirit, brings glory to our Saviour. Paul made this very point to the Christians at Ephesus: 'Let him who stole steal no longer, but rather let him labour, working with his hands what is good, that he may have something to give to him who has need' (Eph. 4:28).

But who should embrace the responsibility of taking the 'unruly' church members to one side in Thessalonica? The **'brethren'** should!

In the same way, those who were fearful about their departed loved ones, or for that matter about their own prospects in the last day, needed not only the comfort and support of the church leadership, but that of the whole fellowship. And what of those believers who struggled to master strong temptation? (People like that often need to be carried.) Let the entire fellowship shoulder the burden of care!

It is worth noting that Paul encouraged his readers to **'be patient'** with everyone, whatever the nature of the problem in each case (5:14). How tempting it can be to throw in the towel! People can be so discouraging. They promise so much, only to disappoint. Nevertheless, we serve a patient Saviour. The church ought never to be the kind of army that shoots its wounded! Verse 15 insists that the local church ought to be a place where kindness flourishes, and not a battleground for the settling of scores!

The local church and its worship (5:16-22)

We come now to Paul's teaching in verses 16-22. It is often supposed that the exhortations in this section are intended as useful pointers to the Christian life in general. Much profit can be gained simply by approaching them on that level. Even so, certain clues contained in the passage suggest that the individual statements hang together as part of a larger whole. A particular theme unifies this section of the epistle, namely the corporate worship of the local church. The reasons for taking this view are as follows:

Firstly, the verbs are in the plural form. In other words, the rejoicing, praying, thanksgiving and so on are to be the actions of a group of people acting together. It goes without saying that the directions given in these verses hold good for believers at any time and in any situation, but this use of plural verb forms suggests strongly that Paul was thinking of the conduct of a gathering of Christians.

Secondly, certain of the things mentioned here only make sense against the background of a number of people assembled together. A kiss of greeting requires at least two people to be present (5:26). More to the point, Paul did not merely want his epistle to be read: it was to be read in the presence of all (5:27). Moreover, the whole matter of testing the utterance of prophets in order to receive whatever was good as from the Lord, while at the same time abstaining from anything which was not, assumes some sort of gathering where those competent to do so could pronounce their verdict on the prophecies in question.

Directives for worship

We have here a number of directives for the conduct of worship. When the Lord's people meet together, each of these components should be present.

1. A joyful church. **'Rejoice always'** (5:16). At this point, the apostle echoes the invitations of the psalmist: 'O come, let us sing to the Lord! Let us shout joyfully to the Rock of our salvation' (Ps. 95:1). 'Make a joyful shout to the Lord, all you lands!' (Ps. 100:1). The reason is simple: as God's people have solid grounds for rejoicing, this note ought to characterize their worship. God has been gracious to us in Christ. Reverence is appropriate because God is so much greater than we are. Flippancy is therefore quite out of order. Even so, reverence does not have to be dour or forbidding.

2. *A prayerful church*. **'Pray without ceasing'** (5:17). The Lord Jesus made the point that it is imperative that his followers should pray and not lose heart (Luke 18:1). This is as important in the corporate life of the church as it is in the private conduct of individual believers. When the first Christians met together, four different aspects of their discipleship had equal weight with them: the apostles' doctrine, fellowship, the breaking of bread and prayer (Acts 2:42). They 'continued steadfastly' in each of these things. The general context strongly suggests that the 'prayer' mentioned here was as much a corporate activity as listening to teaching or participating in the Lord's Supper. In the light of this, it would seem that believers ought to give as prominent a place to corporate prayer as they do to these other things. Sadly the experience of many churches suggests that, with honourable exceptions, this is not generally the case.

3. *A grateful church*. **'In everything give thanks'** (5:18). The background to this exhortation is the fact that the Christian always has good reason to be thankful, even when his outward circumstances are distressing. All things, including those that bring acute distress, are working together for the believer's ultimate benefit (Rom. 8:28-30). On a practical level, this places a burden on the shoulders of those responsible for the conduct of worship services. How can the Lord's people best express this debt of gratitude?

4. *An attentive church*. The people of God must listen to the Word of God (5:19-22). The believers in Thessalonica were warned not to **'quench'** the Holy Spirit. The Spirit of God is often compared with both light and fire. Thus Christians must not douse the light or put out the fire. What does this mean? It is often supposed that Paul's exhortation has something to do

with the exercise of charismatic gifts, particularly because of the reference to prophecies in verse 20. There is no need to restrict the meaning in this way. If we refer back to the verses which immediately precede these words we can see that a failure to rejoice, pray or be thankful would help to extinguish the fire of the Spirit. For that matter, to look back still further, the unruly brothers who would not work, the faint-hearted believers who lacked confidence and those who were prone to give way much too easily in the face of strong temptation all had the effect of throwing a wet blanket over the flames of divine life.

Most of all, the Lord's people run the risk of quenching the Spirit of God when they refuse to give him a hearing. One of the major differences between the churches of the first century and those of today is that we have the enormous blessing of the completed canon of Scripture. The whole of the written Word of God was not available to Christians in Thessalonica, or anywhere else for that matter. Prophets were part of God's provision for the churches of that era. One such person was a man named Agabus, whom we meet on two separate occasions (Acts 11:27-28; 21:10-11). It is sometimes claimed that such prophets are still active in our own time, God having restored them to the churches in recent years. This would be to misunderstand the original role of such God-given prophets. They, along with the apostles, belonged to a period when the Lord was laying the foundation on which the church is built (Eph. 2:20). No additional foundation is necessary. This is not to say that Paul's teaching has nothing to say to believers living near the end of the second millennium. We may not have prophets, but how are we to respond when men occupy the pulpits in our churches and claim that the words they speak are an accurate declaration of the mind of God?

Testing what we hear

Paul recommended intelligent scrutiny. Suppose a man claimed to bring a word from the Lord. What then? To refuse him a hearing might well result in a congregation shutting its ears to God himself. On the other hand, a gullible willingness to credit every self-proclaimed prophet might have the effect of bringing the Lord's people into bondage to something that he had not said and did not require. This explains the two balancing commands: **'Do not despise prophecies'** and **'Test all things'**. In other words, while the believers in Thessalonica should not be in too much of a hurry to silence the person who claimed the gift of prophetic utterance, neither should they be too quick off the mark in taking what he said at face value. Mature reflection was necessary and this often takes time. What kind of tests would be applied?

The first would be *the Scripture test*. Was there any conflict between what the prophet had said and what the Holy Spirit had previously said? Luke commended the fair-minded attitude of the people of Berea (Acts 17:11) who compared Paul's teaching with the written Word of God. This has obvious implications for modern Christians. The preacher who faithfully echoes the truths of the Bible, however modest his gifts as a communicator, deserves our earnest attention. Over against that, the preacher who is at odds with what God has said, however plausible his manner, has no claim on the attention of believers. One thing is vital if individuals and congregations are to function in this way, namely a thorough working knowledge of the Bible.

A second test concerns *the person of Christ*. Does the prophet in question accept the verdict of Scripture concerning the identity of the God-man? What kind of Jesus does he preach? Is it the Christ of Scripture or some other? No one truly inspired by the Spirit of God would deny that Jesus Christ is God the Son, come in human flesh (1 John 4:1-3). After all, the great ministry of the Holy Spirit is to glorify Christ, not to undermine him (John 16:14). In the same way, a prominent clergyman may have his credibility enhanced in the eyes of many because he has been ordained by some avowedly 'Christian' denomination. He may enjoy a measure of respect in the academic community and receive invitations to appear on television chat-shows. Nevertheless, if he preaches any Jesus other than the Jesus of the Bible, true believers would do well to close their ears to him.

In third place, we should also apply *the gospel test*. What does the prophet or teacher say about the way of salvation? If he proclaims a way to heaven other than through the free and sovereign grace of God, a curse rests on his ministry. This applies however exalted the messenger. Even the words of angels need to be weighed and sifted! (Gal. 1:6-9).

Fourthly and finally, we must apply *the test of character*. The character of the prophet would need to be in keeping with his message. The heralds of a holy God should themselves be holy. The passage of twenty centuries has done nothing to make the wolf in sheep's clothing an endangered species.

All of this scrutiny was intended to have a practical outcome. The process of testing resembled the way that a man might check the coins in his pocket to see which were genuine and which were not. Having done so, he would then **'hold fast'** to the good and reject the spurious. In the same way, Christians must actively and energetically pursue what they are taught when it comes from God and decisively shun it when it does not.

9.
Paul prays for his friends

Please read 1 Thessalonians 5:23-28

We have now arrived at the conclusion of Paul's first letter to the believers in Thessalonica. It begins with a double prayer (5:23).

Paul's prayer for his friends (5:23)

Firstly the apostle calls upon God to *sanctify* his friends. Much of the letter has been concerned with the matter of their sanctification. At various points Paul urged his readers to play their part in bringing their lives into line with the will of God. Here he recognizes that the business of ordering our lives as those who are set apart for the service of God will demand more than we can supply. God must work within us if it is to take place at all.

Secondly, Paul asks the Lord to *preserve* his friends in such a manner that when Jesus returns each one would be blameless. The two prayers are connected. Indeed they almost amount to the same idea. If the keeping power of God is to bring believers to the point where the Son of God can find no offence in them when he comes to judge the world in righteousness, this is, in effect, their complete sanctification.

Paul's phrase, **'your whole spirit, soul, and body'**, has been pressed into service in a debate that has raged since the

early centuries of the Christian era about the constitution of
man. Are human beings made up of three component parts, or
merely two? Granted that man has a body, are we to conclude
that the soul and spirit are different names for the non-material
part of his being, or do these words refer to two distinct aspects
of his nature? Elsewhere in the New Testament, Paul consist-
ently argues that there is a dual rather than a triple aspect to the
human constitution (Rom. 8:10; 1 Cor. 5:5; 7:34; 2 Cor. 7:1;
Eph. 2:3; Col. 2:5). In any case, it is not altogether fair to use
this text in such a way. Paul was not attempting to give a
considered judgement on a difficult question about the precise
make-up of human beings: he was praying. And the force of
his prayer was that every part of his friends would be taken up
in the service of God. We must understand his words as an
expression of fervent seriousness. After all, no one takes
Jesus' words in Mark 12:30 about our loving God with all our
heart, soul, mind and strength to mean that man is composed
of four different elements. We are to love God with all that we
are. In the same way, Paul longed that the Lord would deal with
his friends in such a way that they would be able to give their
whole selves to him.

It is not as though the matter was in any doubt, though
Paul's explanation is interesting (5:24). He did not say, 'I am
confident that you will be sanctified and kept because I am
praying for you and prayer is powerful'; his confidence was
built upon the faithfulness of God. True believers last the
course. This is not because they themselves have extraordinary staying power. We Christians are chronically prone to
wander! Our ultimate security rests on the fact that God is
reliable and keeps his promises. He has undertaken to finish
what he starts (Phil. 1:6). Having begun a good work in a
person's life there is no possibility that he will not honour his
commitment and bring everything to a happy conclusion. It is
touching to note that archaeologists have discovered tomb-

stones from Thessalonica marked with the inscription: 'blameless'.

Paul's request for prayer (5:25)

I have no doubt that Paul's touching request for prayer won the hearts of the believers in Thessalonica. For all his achievements he readily admitted that he was as much in need of help as anyone. He had not got beyond the need for prayer. Although he was their spiritual father and teacher, he was on a level with them in one vital respect. He was made of the same fallible human material as the youngest believer in Macedonia and required the help of God as much as they did. And what an encouragement for them to feel that they had a part to play in Paul's ministry, that his success or failure was dependent, at least in part, on their faithfulness in prayer!

How often we forget this! Charles Spurgeon, who preached to 6,000 souls each week during Queen Victoria's heyday, was a man of remarkable gifts. He was also careful to attribute the blessing that came upon his ministry to the fact that his church, the congregation which met in the Metropolitan Tabernacle, gave itself to prayer. The current state of British evangelicalism is directly attributable to the prayer lives of British Christians and the prayer meetings of British churches.

Paul's parting words (5:26-28)

In verse 26 Paul asked that his greetings should be passed on to the whole fellowship. His words are not so much an instruction that the church members should greet each other in a particular way, but more a request of this nature: 'Give all the brothers a kiss for me.' Even so, it seems that exchanging a

'holy kiss', usually at the end of a service, become a recognized custom among the churches. Apparently men kissed
other men and women other women at first, and such kisses
were planted on the cheek of the recipient, but in later years
when men and women exchanged kisses with one another, a
degree of unseemly enthusiasm crept in which had to be
regulated by some of the early church councils. What is
considered an appropriate greeting may well vary from one
culture to another. In some oriental countries bows and other
gestures are made and no physical contact takes place at all.
The important thing, surely, is that we treat our fellow Christians not only with courtesy but with affection according to the
conventions of our own culture.

Paul wanted his letter to be read to the whole fellowship at
Thessalonica (5:27), so much so that the phrase, **'I charge
you,'** is very strong in the original. He put the elders on their
honour to ensure that the letter was read. This is a reflection of
the importance of all that he had written. Whether defending
himself against the accusations of his enemies or instructing
them in vital aspects of Christian truth and conduct, Paul was
a man in earnest. The Christian life is not for dabblers.

Charles Simeon, vicar of Holy Trinity Church in Cam-
bridge during the early years of the nineteenth century, had a
profound effect on a whole generation of Anglican clergymen.
In his home he kept a portrait of Henry Martyn, a pioneer
missionary to the Muslim world. Simeon confessed that when
he looked at the picture he felt that the young evangelist's eyes
never left him, as though they were silently urging him to
greater seriousness. If the portrait could have spoken it would
have said, 'Don't trifle, don't trifle!' What was Simeon's
response? 'And I won't trifle! I won't trifle!'

The letter ends as it began, with a prayer that all who read
it might experience the grace of God.

2 Thessalonians

10.
Why did Paul write
2 Thessalonians?

The second letter to the Christians in Thessalonica followed hard on the heels of the first. We learn from Acts 20 that Paul eventually went back to Macedonia, so it seems likely that this letter was written before that return journey. It is probable that Paul wrote the second epistle little more than a few weeks after the first, while he was still in Corinth with Timothy and Silas.

There is one obvious point of difference between the two letters. In 2 Thessalonians Paul has nothing to say in defence of his character and conduct. We can safely assume that the lengthy treatment which he had given this matter in the first epistle had silenced his critics. Paul did, however, feel it necessary to return to two of the subjects which he had raised in the first letter.

The last things

First of all, it appears that some of the believers in Thessalonica still faced nagging fears about the last things. They were in danger of being deceived (2:3). Paul's language suggests that certain false teachings were circulating and that those responsible had passed their notions off as coming from Paul

himself (2:2). This explains why the second main section of
the epistle (2:1-17) is devoted to further teaching on 'the
coming of our Lord Jesus Christ and our gathering together to
him' (2:1). In particular, the apostle answers a charge which
will seem strange to modern readers, namely that the Second
Coming had already taken place (2:2). This led him to observe
that this glorious event will be heralded by the arrival of 'the
man of sin'. What follows is one of the clearest portions of
Scripture with respect to the identity and prospects of this
individual. To a generation of Christians who are almost two
thousand years closer to the end, this section cannot be other
than enormously helpful.

Those who were idle

Paul also returned to another matter which had occupied him
during the first epistle. A section of the church membership in
Thessalonica had been causing concern because of their
idleness, probably justifying their refusal to work by appeal-
ing to the nearness of Christ's return. It would seem that things
had not improved, for in his third main section of this second
letter (3:6-15), Paul spoke even more forcefully than he had
the first time round. The tone of some of his remarks suggests
that the problem was so deep-rooted that he was contemplat-
ing the grim possibility of church discipline.

Enduring persecution

The first letter also contained references to the fact that the
church in Thessalonica had experienced persecution. At times
this had been very severe. It would seem that word had got
back to Paul that this opposition had provoked a bout of heart-

searching. Why did God allow it? Throughout the twenty centuries of the Christian era, the sufferings of the godly have led them to question the justice of God. Paul's concern in the first section of the epistle (1:3-12) was to address this very issue.

11.
Opening greeting and thanksgiving

Please read 2 Thessalonians 1:1-5

Paul's greeting (1:1-2)

Paul's opening salutation is almost word for word the same as the one which marks the beginning of the previous epistle. The only difference is that the church in Thessalonica is described as being **'in God our Father'** rather than 'in God the Father of our Lord Jesus Christ'. The emphasis is not only on the fact that believers have been adopted into the family of God, but also, by his use of the word 'our', that Paul associated himself completely with his brothers and sisters in Thessalonica.

Paul's prayer of thanksgiving (1:3-4)

In these verses, Paul gave heartfelt thanks to God for all that his grace has achieved in his friends (1:3-4). The apostle felt that he and his fellow-workers were under an obligation to thank God for the spiritual progress made by the believers in Macedonia. The word **'bound'** suggests that they were under compulsion, as though the Lord had done something so notable in the lives of these Christians that it would be churlish not to give thanks. The second expression, **'as it is fitting'**, suggests that this gratitude was no more and no less than was due. Thanksgiving was, as we might say, 'only right and proper'. Three things stood out.

1. The growth of their faith

The word **'exceedingly'** should have its full weight. Paul meant to convey the idea that growth had been outstanding. Every time their faith had been put to the test, they had found that God could be trusted. This in turn encouraged them to rely on him all the more. Such a spectacular improvement must have encouraged the apostle, for in the earlier letter he had expressed a desire to help in making up what was lacking in their faith (1 Thess. 3:10).

Modern people are apt to suppose that faith is like red hair or freckles, a random affair that some have and others do not. For instance, Christians often hear friends say things like, 'I wish I had your faith', as if they had missed out in some way. The correct reply to such a statement would run like this: 'Why won't you trust my Saviour? Is there something about him that has convinced you that he cannot be trusted?'

These first-century Christians are a spur to us because their faith was not static.

2. The growth of their love for each other

The mutual love of these Macedonian Christians was impressive. Love was evident throughout the whole fellowship. Everyone practised it and everyone received it. People with a lot in common often get on. A shared interest, whether it be flower arranging or photography, helps to overcome our inhibitions and create a bond. Christian love, however, ought to be far more than the natural affinity of the 'in-group'. What keeps some churches together? If it is little more than a shared liking for austere worship, lengthy sermons and Puritan books (or any other brand of evangelical culture, for that matter), the church in question is little more than a kind of religious club. If, on the other hand, people are drawn together because they see in each other a powerful sense of attraction to Jesus Christ, they have the beginnings of the kind of love that should mark a Christian church. This love will unite people who would otherwise have little in common: professional people and those who depend on state benefits, highbrow and lowbrow, the boisterous extrovert and the painfully shy, folk with sophisticated tastes and those with no taste whatsoever!

Paul thanked God because he could see something happening in Thessalonica that amounted to a miracle. The gospel had brought people together who would normally have avoided one another. It is vital that Christians pray that love of this kind would permeate our churches to an increasing measure, for when love begins to diminish, friction increases and churches fall apart. When Christians quarrel or fellowships divide it is too easy to put it all down to a point of principle, to assume, for instance, that people have taken sides over a doctrinal issue. The issue in question, however, could often prompt us to ask, 'Why does this matter more to you than your brother who loves Jesus at least as well as you do?'

3. Their endurance under pressure

Paul took great encouragement from the way that his friends bore up under **'persecutions and tribulations'**. He was so impressed by their steadfastness that he talked about it approvingly among the other churches. The word **'boast'** does not mean that he claimed the credit for their achievements ('Look what a great church I've planted!'). It was more that he felt that this quality of patience in adversity was solid proof that God was at work in their lives.

In some circles nowadays it is actively taught that material wealth and physical well-being are the outward marks of spiritual prosperity. Paul would have had no sympathy with this kind of thinking. He prized Christians who could hold up when the going got rough because they knew that suffering was not a sign that the Lord had abandoned them, but proof positive that they were following in the steps the Master trod. Jesus warned his disciples that 'A servant is not greater than his master. If they persecuted me, they will also persecute you. If they kept my word, they will keep yours also' (John 15:20).

Paul's attitude towards these Christians can teach us a great deal. What do we appreciate? Those things which make us feel grateful will reveal a great deal about our hearts; they will tell us where our priorities truly lie. So often we are thankful for things that make for our comfort or our financial security. Paul gave thanks for a group of people. Even at this point, his priorities challenge ours. What is it about other people that we value most? Ask parents how their children are coming along and you will often be told about exam results or career prospects. Paul was grateful to God for people who were making spiritual progress.

What is the best way to encourage a Christian? The last thing that we want to do is pander to a believer's pride. Unfortunately this sometimes puts us in a quandary. If we thank people for the contribution that they have made to the life of their church, or for something that has been of real personal help, might this not lead in turn to a bloated ego? On the other hand, if we say nothing at all, might this not have the equally unhappy effect of leaving them feeling unappreciated? Paul's method has much to commend it. He thanked God for his friends' growth and Christian maturity. This avoided the danger, on the one hand, of their feeling that their efforts counted for nothing and, on the other hand, of encouraging them to think that they had a right to claim the credit for the work of God in their lives.

12.
The justice of God

Please read 2 Thessalonians 1:5-10

When godly people suffer, they are often tempted to call the justice of God into question. Those who suffer are those who deserve it least, while the undeserving do as they please and are not called to account for it. Paul's concern was to help his friends keep their spiritual balance in the face of such temptations.

To begin with, he made the point that their very patience was itself **'manifest evidence of the righteous judgement of God'** (1:5). What was it that kept them going, if not the conviction that God's cause was right and that he would vindicate them in his own time?

There is also a strong hint here of the teaching found elsewhere in the New Testament that suffering is a 'given' in the Christian life. Jesus himself taught that the way of the cross is the pattern for the follower of Jesus as much as for the Master (Mark 8:31-38) and Paul taught that we enter the kingdom of God through 'many tribulations' (Acts 14:22).

What should believers do when they suffer for the sake of the gospel? They should begin by reminding themselves that their experience does not support the idea that something has gone wrong, but rather that their discipleship is authentic. They can be **'counted worthy of the kingdom of God'**, not in the sense that they deserve their place in it, but rather that they can rest content that there is convincing evidence that their Christianity is genuine.

The main thrust of Paul's case, however, is that Christians must learn to take the long view. Does the Almighty deal justly in his treatment of those who love him and those who defy him? The apostle bids us consider the approaching end of human history (1:6-7). When that day dawns there will be no lingering doubts about the way that God has dealt with mankind.

All of this is closely linked with the revelation of Jesus Christ. Jesus will be **'revealed'** in the same way that a statue is unveiled. What was once hidden from sight will be in the full view of all. The unbelieving world has mocked the hope of Christians for years. Why put your trust in someone when you have no guarantee that he is even there? Believers for their part have had to live with the frustration that, though convinced of the reality of Jesus, they have not been able to silence the cynics. But scoffers will find that every taunt will die on their lips when the one who has been concealed stands revealed in all his splendour.

What will the last day in the history of our planet be like? We can make two observations.

It will be a day of vindication

Christians have been on the receiving end for twenty centuries. The passing generations have all wondered whether God has allowed the wicked to get away with their oppression. Now, at last, the settling of accounts will take place. Those who trouble believers will be paid back in their own coin, and in full (1:6). Believers themselves will see an end to their trials. The long years of oppression will be over; they will be able to 'rest' and be at peace. Does the Christian life seem an unequal struggle against unremitting odds? Cheer up, Jesus is coming to the rescue!

For the believer, the day of Jesus' return will be the best of days, 'our day'. That is because the end also marks a new

beginning. The heavens and earth which now exist will be
replaced by something far better (2 Peter 3:13). The voice that
summons mankind to judgement also speaks the thrilling
words: 'Behold, I make all things new!' (Rev. 21:5). The new
heavens and new earth will have a completely different
character to the old. They will be the home of 'righteousness'.
Moral soundness will pervade every nook and cranny of the
world to come. What a contrast with the present state of things!
In effect, the holocaust of the end will act like a blast furnace
where all the impurities in the metal are burned off. All the
devastating effects of the Fall will be purged away. How
chafing it is to live in a world where evil is never completely
subdued! The child of God aches for a home where there are
no drug pushers, rapists, muggers and paedophiles, no cynical
politicians or aggressive military dictatorships. Indeed he
sighs for a future where he will not be vexed by the contrary
impulses of his own heart. The glorious news is that such a
world will one day be the Christian's home. A golden future
has been promised, the truly just society which generations of
philosophers and politicians have failed to produce.

The day of the Lord is a day to quicken the pulse of any
believer. At last, God will extirpate all moral evil, root and
branch, from the universe. The prospect before us is of a world
without pain. Human bodies will not sicken or decay. No
funerals will take place. There will be no crime and therefore
none of the debilitating fear of crime which saps the morale of
modern society. Environmental damage will be no more;
sadness will have been abolished. When tears are shed they
will be tears of joy and laughter. God himself will be at home
in that world, content to live among a people who bask in his
glorious presence. He and they together will be suffused with
joy too rich for human language. Nothing can spoil that future,
for all that was evil has been consigned to the furnace. I ask you
to picture a future as lovely as Christ himself and then to ask
yourself whether you will have a part in it.

What will happen when the Lord of glory finally arrives?

1. He will 'be glorified in his saints' (1:10)

Not only will he affirm them, honour them, vindicate them and proclaim before angels and men that they are his, but he will bestow his glory upon them so that they are transformed by it. The people of God will be lit up with glory; they will glow with his radiance. Samuel Rutherford, the eminent Scottish minister of the seventeenth century, was once asked, 'What will Christ be like when he cometh?' The answer that he gave was: 'All lovely'. Paul wanted his friends in Thessalonica to appreciate that the loveliness of Jesus would become theirs in such a way that they would become lovely too. When the Son of God finally appears, his people not only have the enticing prospect of seeing him as he is, but of being like him (1 John 3:2).

2. He will 'be admired among all those who believe'

The waiting multitudes of Christian people will gasp in delighted astonishment. Jesus will exceed all their expectations. There will not be room in a single believing heart for disappointment. Every one of them will be thrilled with his magnificence. As they reflect upon the ages that preceded his coming, their verdict will be that the wait was long, but that he was worth waiting for!

It will be a day of vengeance

What will become of those people who have lived so as to become worthy targets for divine retribution? They are described in two ways.

1. They are those 'who do not know God' (1:8)

Do you know God? We cannot overstate the importance of such a relationship. Jesus himself said that eternal life depends on our knowing God and Jesus Christ whom he has sent (John 17:3). Everything hangs on it. To know God is to be secure for eternity; to be a stranger to him is to face the certain prospect of eternal misery. We must not think of the plight of such people as a random misfortune. I only heard Dr Martyn Lloyd-Jones preach on two occasions. Though I relished the thought of a few moments' conversation with the great man, in the event I did not manage to shake his hand at the conclusion of either service. Such things are commonly put down to 'bad luck': the building was crammed, it just wasn't my day! Those who do not know God, however, are not people who have missed out on an introduction through no fault of their own. They are in that position because they have steadfastly refused to have anything to do with him. In effect, they have banished God from their lives. They will get their due reward when they are banished from his presence for ever (1:9).

2. They 'do not obey the gospel' (1:8)

Does this sound strange? Do we think it should read, 'those who do not believe the gospel'? In point of fact, the gospel message makes demands upon us. A response is required. We cannot see the kingdom of God unless we undergo an experience called the new birth (John 3:3). Have we been born again? In the same way, Jesus insists that admittance into the kingdom of heaven is only for those who have been converted (Matt. 18:3). Have we been converted? God calls on everyone throughout the world to repent (Acts 17:30). Have we made a positive response to that call? How can we be saved from the awful prospect of eternal destruction? (1:9). The answer is that we must 'believe on the Lord Jesus Christ' if we are to be saved (Acts 16:31). How many of us have obeyed that instruction?

We must never speak lightly of the vengeance of God. The reality is terrifying. It amounts to **'everlasting destruction from the presence of the Lord'**. The idea of conscious, never-ending torment is clearly so dreadful that we shrink from it. Some scholars have allowed their horror at the idea to get the better of them to such an extent that they argue that the Bible does not teach it. Some of them have used Paul's phrase 'everlasting destruction' to support their views. If a thing is destroyed, surely that is an end of it? The English, however, translates a Greek word which means that the thing in question is not so much obliterated as ruined. It becomes the wreck of what it once was. This destruction is linked with the fact that the souls in question are cut off from the presence of God. Just as the believer finds his true humanity through union with Christ, the unrepentant sinner will be separated from the source of all good and ultimately from the fountain of true personality. Through contact with his Saviour, the justified sinner will open like a flower and grow in radiant splendour. Denied that contact, the unbeliever will wither and fade. Hell is full of the debris of humanity!

As that fateful day approaches, we live in a world where big things are at stake. We are surrounded by people hurtling towards a destiny too horrible to contemplate. As believers, it is our duty to try to arrest them in their headlong flight and confront them with the claims of Christ. Paul saw this as a colossal responsibility. That is why he prayed for his friends. Should we not pray for one another?

13.
Paul prays for his friends once more

Please read 2 Thessalonians 1:11-12

As a teenager, I dreaded the annual ordeal of the school speech day. The largest theatre in the borough was hired for the occasion, a combination of prize-giving, musical recital and an attempt to rally the troops with stirring speeches. (In the event, we always felt more patronized than inspired.) For weeks beforehand, music lessons were entirely given over to practising the school song, a rousing rendition of which was supposed to be the thrilling climax to a glorious occasion. If ever there was a futile exercise, it must be the effort of trying to persuade several hundred teenage boys to sing their school song with conviction! Far from joining in with loyal gusto, we often concocted our own anarchic parodies of it. I understand that a leading British public school has a song called 'Forty years on'. Pupils are asked to think about the memories they will have as they look back on their school careers from the vantage point of middle age. Will they recall those days with a sense of achievement or regret? Paul had something similar in mind when he wrote to his friends in Thessalonica. Events were unfolding which would soon usher in the daunting prospect of eternity. Forty million years down the road, how would they view the lives that they had lived while on earth? Would it be a tale of wasted opportunities, or a period of preparation for the life to come? Conscious that the end of all things was approaching, Paul prayed for his friends. The content of his prayer is worth exploring in detail.

He prayed that God would count them worthy of their calling

The apostle's starting-point was that each of his readers had responded to the call of God (1:11). In Paul's thinking, that call is dynamic. On the one hand, it is an invitation from a crucified Saviour. It has the irresistible drawing power of unconquerable love. On the other hand, it comes as a summons from the throne room of the universe, a powerful word of command which overcomes all human resistance. It is a noble calling. It demands that we have done with moral evil and with mediocrity; it calls us to a life of holy excellence. It is summed up in the idea of following Jesus. A call like that would demand all that the Thessalonian Christians could give and more! That is why Paul made it his regular practice to pray that God would count them worthy of it. In effect, this meant that he asked God to work within them in such a way that their lives would increasingly bring credit to the great God who called them.

They were certainly not worthy when they first heard the call of Christ! It is the same for all believers. The gospel invitation does not come to those who deserve it, but to people who defy God and live as though he did not exist. Furthermore, in praying that God would count the believers in Thessalonica worthy of the call which he had issued, Paul did not mean that his friends might eventually reach the stage where they did merit his attention. It was a plea that God would make his friends what they had not been before. In effect, it was a prayer for spiritual growth so that their lives would not bring shame upon the gospel. The apostle had already noted their growing faith and abundant love (5:3); now he prayed that these things would grow yet more. His great longing was to see the development of Christian character so that when the time came for the great division of mankind into the saved and the lost, no one would be in any doubt as to which camp these folk belonged to.

Why did Paul make this a matter for prayer? Why not content himself with a challenge to the Thessalonian believers along these lines: 'Be worthy of this calling! Work harder, improve, be more committed!'? (In point of fact, he did issue a challenge of this nature to the Christians at Ephesus — see Eph. 4:1). Paul prayed, however, because they were made of the same stuff as you and I are. Left to ourselves, the task is too great. We are called to resemble Christ. How can we do that without his help? By all means, let us pray for one another!

So often when we pray for others, our focus is not on the people themselves but on the things they have (or don't have) or their personal circumstances. Will Tom be cured of his illness? Will Jenny get that job, or the grades she needs to get into college? In the same way, when we pray for ourselves, we tend to seek an escape route from unpleasant situations. This kind of thing is not altogether wrong, but Paul had something else in mind. He was not so much concerned with asking God to smooth their path, but with what he would make them. Think of the people that you often pray for. Do you ask the Lord to do nice things for them, or to make them shining examples of the power of grace?

He prayed that God would bring them to the point where their living and praying were in harmony with his will

Paul's second prayer is breathtaking. It is often supposed that the **'good pleasure'** mentioned here is a reference to the will of God. It seems likely, however, that Paul has something else in mind, firstly because all prayer is offered against the backdrop of the sovereign purposes of the Almighty, and secondly because Paul's primary concern in this prayer was that God would do something in the lives of his friends. In other words, he prayed 'that God, by his great power, would fulfil all your good pleasure and work of faith'. Does this mean that the apostle expected the Almighty to give his friends what they wanted? In one sense, that was precisely what he did mean. It was not that he saw the Almighty as first cousin to Aladdin's genie of the lamp, the immortal obliged to do the bidding of mere mortals: 'Your wish is my command, O master!' Paul did not request a blank cheque for his friends. There is an important rider. May God bring their plans and activities to fruition when they are prompted by faith! At the core of Paul's thinking lies the notion that people who are truly converted have a different set of goals and ambitions from those who are not. Christians, at least in measure, will want what God wants. Consider the opening petitions of the Lord's Prayer. The hallowing of God's name, the extension of his kingdom and the triumph of his will on this rebellious earth are all issues that lie close to the heart of God. Something is wrong if these things do not matter to us too.

God will not underwrite our plans when these are driven by a desire for our own enrichment, comfort or convenience. Paul envisages something else. Because the Spirit of God is at work within us, our aspirations are increasingly shaped by his priorities. Are there ways in which I could be a more loving father, supportive wife, conscientious church member? Is there something practical I can do to bring the gospel to my neighbours? And when we pray for others who have re-sponded to the promptings of faith with action, why not be confident? If our friends are truly in tune with the mind of Christ, our Saviour has a stake in the outcome. Suppose we are concerned to share the gospel with others. Is it unreasonable to expect help from above? Do we have more of a heart for the lost than the Father who loved the world and sent his Son to save those who believe, or than the Son who wept over hard-hearted Jerusalem and the Spirit who continually strives with unyielding human hearts?

Two important considerations lie just below the surface.

First of all, given that Paul prayed for the blessing of God on all that his friends wanted to achieve for the gospel, this necessarily means that the people in question needed help to live as close to the Lord as possible. This was vital if they were to think and feel as he thinks and feels. When you are aware of a Christian friend who is setting out do something worthwhile for God, he needs your prayers. He needs the blessing of the Almighty on his endeavours, but he also needs to live near to his Master's heart. That is the only way to ensure that his vision truly stems from God and is not a grandiose dream of his own imagining.

Secondly, can we really be sure about our own agendas? We pray that the Lord would bless our service and we covet the prayers of others, but can we be sure of our motives? How far are our activities truly the result of faith?

He prayed that Jesus would be glorified in them and they in him

Another element in Paul's unceasing prayer for his friends in Thessalonica is 'glory' (1:12). One thing mattered over and above everything else: the glory of Jesus. This involves more than ending our prayers by saying, '… in Jesus' name, Amen,' or 'We ask this for your glory.' These phrases are often repeated merely for form's sake. What really matters is the spirit which animates all our praying. The apostle's petitions were shot through with requests that the eternal Father would promote the reputation of his Son. This outcome mattered more than anything else. What a challenge! When we pray for brother X, it is he who fills our thoughts. We have his interests in mind. Suppose instead that the glory of our Saviour is uppermost in our prayers, so that we beg God the Father to glorify his Son in the life of our brother. Are we ready for all that might ensue? The Lord has a way of magnifying Jesus by showing his power in situations of human weakness. Sometimes a terrible price has to be paid in suffering to provide the backdrop against which the grace and power of Christ are displayed.

Paul mentions the glory of Christ at this point partly to correct any possibility of misunderstanding over his earlier remarks about the Lord bringing our plans to fruition. How well do we know ourselves? Even spiritual ministry can be undertaken out of a desire for self-promotion. The pastor wants a growing church so that he will not feel a failure; sister Y supports the open-air services because she wants to be well thought of among the people at church who really matter. Our service for God can rapidly become a form of idolatry. We don't so much worship God as our preaching, or whatever task we do in the life of the church. Zealous Christians need prayer that God would keep them from themselves! Paul's concern was that the Thessalonian believers would be transparent and that the glory of Christ would shine through. What about the dynamic Christian worker? People stand in awe of his verve and commitment. His untiring labours leave everyone breathless with admiration while his gifts are almost proverbial. Even so, as M'Cheyne said, 'It is not great talents that God blesses, so much as great likeness to Jesus.' How do we pray for our friends? Do we ask that God would give them a savour of Christ?

It may be surprising that the apostle should go on to pray that his friends should be glorified too. Does this mean that provided we give our Saviour his due, a little self-promotion is acceptable? Not at all. There is a marked difference between our glorifying God and his glorifying us. When we give glory to God, we simply give him what is his by right. To do anything else is actually to rob him. He is glorious and deserves to have this fact recognized. When God glorifies us, he bestows something that we do not deserve. The glorification of a Christian is not a statement about the person's worth or merits, but about the kindness of a generous God who lavishes love upon the undeserving. At this stage, Paul principally has the end in view, the undying, never-ending beauty which will belong to every child of God when our Saviour returns in **'the glory of his power'** (1:9). It echoes an earlier prayer of Jesus himself (see John 17:24). Nevertheless, it actually begins in this life. Elsewhere Paul speaks of Christians being changed 'from glory into glory' as they learn increasingly to fix their eyes on Jesus (2 Cor. 3:18). Here is another spur to our prayers. Oh that God would help our brothers and sisters increasingly to 'seek those things which are above, where Christ is'! (Col. 3:1).

Some Christians pray in a way which suggests that, for them, the whole exercise is somewhat speculative: 'Try it — who knows, it might just work!' If you are sometimes tempted to pray in that kind of spirit, take a long, thoughtful look at the apostle at prayer. Was he in two minds about the outcome? Certainly he was clear about his objectives. He knew what really mattered. Best of all, however, he knew what kind of God he was dealing with. The backdrop to all his praying was **'the grace of our God and the Lord Jesus Christ'**. Our God is kind. He showers mercy on pitiful specimens like us. Not only can he 'do exceedingly abundantly above all that we ask or think' (Eph. 3:20), but he has a mind to do so!

14.
The rebellion of Antichrist

Please read 2 Thessalonians 2:1-17

A warning against false teachers (2:1-3)

Paul was concerned. Some of his friends in Thessalonica had evidently got hold of the idea that **'the day of Christ had come'**. It is hard to square this with Paul's earlier teaching about the nature of that awesome day in 1 Thessalonians. How could anyone jump to the conclusion that it had already taken place and they had somehow managed to miss it? Could anything be a bigger tragedy than to live out one's days altogether unaware that the conclusion of human history had taken place? Perhaps some had been taken in by this notion because the rumour was going around that Paul himself was the source of this teaching. The false teachers who were circulating the idea that Jesus had already returned obviously understood that this teaching would seem much more plausible if they could lay it all at his door. It was all deliberately vague. Instead of any concrete explanation, three different suggestions had been put forward. Firstly, it had come to Paul in **'spirit'** — in other words, he had received a revelation. Secondly, it was suggested that he had spoken on the subject, that a verbal message from him (a **'word'**) was going the rounds. Finally, it was also argued that a **'letter'** from Paul was circulating among the churches. Paul urged his friends not to become excited by all of this speculation. He was emphatically not responsible for the rumours that had caused the believers such heartache.

Even in the late twentieth century, the idea that Christ's return is now a thing of the past has its supporters. The movement now known as the Jehovah's Witnesses originally gained a hearing for themselves with the confident assertion of their founder, Pastor Charles T. Russell, that Christ would come again in 1875. When that year passed in much the same fashion as 1874, some hasty readjustments were called for. It was decreed that the relevant prophecies had been sifted and that a more reliable calculation prompted the movement to adopt the revised date of 1914. Even though this year was notable for the great cataclysm of World War I, nothing resembling the 'day of the Lord' took place. In order to rescue the battered credibility of the movement, the new leader, Judge J. F. Rutherford, declared in 1916 that Christ had returned in 1914 after all, but that it was an invisible coming — he had come unobserved!

Paul's message was that the Christians in Thessalonica could put their minds at rest. Not only could they rest assured that the end had not come and gone unnoticed, they could also tell themselves that they, unlike some (1 Thess. 5:2-4) would not be caught unawares. The end is now 2,000 years nearer than it was when Paul set out to reassure his friends. How much time remains? Whether it amounts to months, decades or centuries, Paul would have us understand that something must happen first which will serve as a dramatic warning to the Lord's people. This great preliminary event amounts to a **'falling away'**. This translates a Greek word which can also be rendered 'rebellion'. Presiding over it all, an individual named the **'man of sin'** will emerge. At this point, Paul introduces us to the person whom the apostle John names 'the Antichrist' (1 John 2:18).

The character of Antichrist (2:3-4)

The word 'antichrist' is enough in itself to send a shiver down the spine. Paul's description leaves us in no doubt that the last days of our planet will be dominated by a figure of towering evil. How are we to recognize him when he comes? Paul builds up a composite picture of him, layer by layer. Four different terms are used to portray this monster:

1. He is 'the man of sin' (2:3)

Some versions of the Bible render this as 'the man of lawlessness'. His opposition to God reveals itself through his contempt for all that is holy. He rejects morality and denies the validity of any kind of ethical restraint whatever. The phrase 'man of sin' is a typically Hebrew way of indicating that this man is evil to the core. In just the same way that God is described as the 'Father of lights' (James 1:17), which means that there is nothing morally dubious in his entire being, so the leader of the last rebellion against God will be a person devoid of any shred of respect for the law of God.

2. He is 'the son of perdition' (2:3)

'Perdition' is nowadays a somewhat archaic term. It means 'lostness'. The Antichrist is doomed. For all the fact that he is destined to enjoy a spectacular rise to power and a brief period of ghastly prominence, eternal ruin lies in wait for him. Lawlessness is his nature, destruction is his destiny.

3. He is the opponent of God (2:4)

Everything that belongs to God comes within the range of his malice. God himself, the gospel and the church are all the objects of his hate-filled campaign.

4. He is consumed with pride (2:4)

Paul tells us that he **'exalts himself'**. He is the great egotist. He wishes to occupy the highest place of all and makes it his ambition to take the place of God in the hearts and minds of men. He covets nothing short of worship, usurping the throne of God in the very temple.

At this point, Paul echoes the prophecy of Daniel. Daniel had warned of an act of defiance against God so terrible that he called it 'the abomination of desolation' (Dan. 11:31; 12:11). His prediction came true, at least in part, in the year 169 B.C. The Syrian king, Antiochus IV, captured Jerusalem and deliberately desecrated the temple by entering the Most Holy Place. The next year he added to his calculated insult against the Almighty by building an altar to the god Zeus on the altar of burnt offering and sacrificing a pig on it. It is hard to imagine anything more offensive to the religious sensitivities of the Jewish people. It would seem likely that Paul is referring back to Daniel's prophecy and to this incident, suggesting that the Antichrist will deliberately defy the living God by asserting that he deserves the worship that belongs to God alone. This is why I am convinced that the 'man of sin' and Antichrist are the same person.

In modern English, the Greek prefix 'anti-' is employed to convey the idea of opposition. Anti-aircraft guns destroy enemy aircraft, anti-histamine ointment counteracts the irritation caused by insect bites. This idea is obviously part of the thinking behind the name 'Antichrist'. He is the implacable foe of the true Christ. The Greek term, however, also includes the idea of substitution, one who takes the place of another, in this case for evil motives. Antichrist pretends to be Christ; he is a counterfeit Messiah. The temple that Paul knew is no more. Instead we are invited to consider a man so consumed by the spirit of rebellion that he mounts a campaign of subversion, attempting to seize control of the professing church.

In the summer of 1936, the country of Spain was rent by civil war. The leading army officers had been plotting for months to seize power and replace the republican government with a fascist dictatorship. They had hoped that meticulous planning and the element of surprise would give them complete victory in a matter of days. In the event, war dragged on for three blood-soaked years, because the fascist generals failed to capture Madrid, the capital city and seat of government. Even so, in July 1936 the odds seemed stacked in their favour. The world's press hovered like vultures. One newspaperman gained an interview with the fascist general Emilio Mola and asked him how he intended to seize Madrid. The general said that five columns were about to mount their assault. The journalist was puzzled: he could only see four. General Mola replied that the fifth column was inside the city, a group of fascist sympathizers was ready to undermine the efforts of the defenders. Ever since that time, the phrase 'fifth column' has been used to describe the enemy within.

In the same way, the Christian church does not merely have to contend with the attacks of enemies on the outside. Communists used used to boast that they looked forward to the day when the Christian cause would be extinguished, snuffed out like a candle. At least their opposition was frank and open. Far more harm has been done down the centuries by movements which have made subversion their goal. They have pretended to be Christian, while undermining the church from within. I do not expect to see Antichrist arise from within some avowedly non-Christian movement, whether Communism, Islam, or any other such grouping. Instead, I believe that he will prove to be the arch fifth-columnist. He will masquerade as a Christian leader, perhaps even as Christ himself.

All along, I have assumed that Paul has a person in mind, rather than an institution, organization or movement. His language describes the attitude and behaviour of a person. At this point we would do well not to attempt a detailed assessment of his identity. At various times in history, wicked men have arisen who have behaved like Antiochus IV. It has been enormously tempting for Christians alive at such times to conclude that Antichrist had at last been revealed. It should not surprise us that Christians who experienced terrible persecution at the hands of the Roman Catholic hierarchy concluded that one or other of the popes of the period, or perhaps the papacy as an institution, was the Antichrist. The *Westminster Confession* and the *Baptist Confession of 1689* both contain statements to this effect. It is however, a little premature to identify the 'man of lawlessness' with a particular pope. We must not forget that John wrote that 'many antichrists' have already come (1 John 2:18). It is as though we can expect a succession of men who embody evil in themselves, with the worst and most terrible of them all making his appearance immediately before the end of all things.

The restraining of Antichrist (2:5-8)

Paul goes on to explain that the Antichrist is being held back; a restraining power is at work which prevents his being revealed. There is some ambiguity here because in verse 6 the word **'what'** suggests that Paul was referring to a force, whereas in verse 7 the word **'he'** suggests that he had a person in mind. What did Paul mean? We cannot be absolutely certain, but the suggestion which seems most convincing is that the power of government is holding the advance of the great rebellion in check for the time being. My reasons for adopting this suggestion are as follows:

1. Paul taught elsewhere (Rom. 13:1-5) that the governments of civil societies are not so much an accidental by-product of their historical development as

a blessing bestowed by God himself. Moreover, the 'powers that be' were ordained by God for the specific purpose of restraining evil. What prevents the man of lawlessness from emerging onto the scene in all his dreadful pomp? The power of law.

2. This interpretation fits in well with Paul's own experience. There had been occasions when what had stood between him and an ugly fate had been the strong arm of the Roman state. This letter was written from Corinth. While resident in that city, Paul had been the victim of a plot concocted by certain members of the local Jewish community (Acts 18:12-16). The apostle came through it all because of the scrupulous fairness of the Roman proconsul, a man named Gallio. In later years, he was to undergo a similar experience when he almost suffered death at the hands of a Jewish lynch-mob in the precincts of the temple in Jerusalem. He kept his hide intact because of the swift intervention of Roman soldiers (Acts 21:26-36).

3. The neutral expression in verse 6, **'what is restraining'**, and the personal reference in verse 7, **'he who restrains'**, need not present a problem if we bear in mind the fact that states are often personified by reference to their rulers. In modern Britain, just as in ancient Rome, the Crown, or the monarch herself, is often used as a shorthand way of referring to the whole apparatus of government. Republics often use the same kind of device by referring to the president or the equivalent head of state.

None of this is to say that government is an unmixed blessing. Because politicians, like the rest of us, are members of a fallen race, we who must bear the consequences of their decisions will often find that there is much to lament as well as much for which we thank God. At times certain states fall under the control of wicked individuals, or groups which subscribe to evil philosophies. Nevertheless, as a general observation, the rule of law is preferable to anarchy. A tentative reconstruction of Paul's scenario would therefore suggest that at present, the power of lawlessness is **'already at work'**, but much of its activity is behind the scenes, Satan, the sponsor of the rebellion, cannot achieve all that he would like because, in spite of the damage caused by the Fall, the God-given instruments of law and order which still exist in human society, though in varying degrees in different parts of the world, hold him in check. The apostle, however, envisages a time when the rule of law is increasingly held in contempt, moral absolutes are derided and the institutions that civilized nations have used to restrain the effects of the innate evil that lurks within the human heart can no longer perform their appointed task. Just as the dykes which the Dutch people used to construct to keep the sea at bay would sometimes give way before the relentless power of the ocean, so the bulwarks which keep evil in check in human societies will eventually collapse before the flood-tide of wickedness. It is at such a time that the captain of the great rebellion will be revealed for what he is. Does the thought of this individual send a shiver down the spine? It is only natural that the people of God should anticipate such events with a sense of foreboding. Even so, a sense of proportion is required. Christians are often tempted to fall into an attitude known as 'dualism', the idea that the powers of light and darkness are evenly matched and that if God wins out over the devil at all, it will only be by dint of hard struggle. The Scripture insists that Satan's great captain will melt like snow in the fiery heat of the wrath of the coming Christ. In the event, he will be no match at all for the splendid conqueror who **'will consume [him] with the breath of his mouth'**. To quote Martin Luther, 'A word shall quickly slay him!'

Antichrist and his followers (2:9-12).

The coming of the lawless one will be a stern test for those people who are alive at the time. He will be plausible. All the indications are that he will be a miracle-worker. This should not surprise us. His great goal is to persuade mankind to worship him. One of the stratagems that he will employ with this in mind is a programme of deceptive miracles. In this respect, the coming of the man of sin will be a kind of ghastly parody of the coming of Christ. In his sermon on the Day of Pentecost, the apostle Peter spoke of 'Jesus of Nazareth, a man attested by God to you by miracles, wonders and signs' (Acts 2:22). In a similar way, the Antichrist will appear in person and his appearance will be authenticated by the miraculous. He will have a battery of signs and wonders which are all intended to trick people into thinking that he is genuine.

His wonders are **'lying'** (2:9) not so much in the sense that they are fakes, but rather the point is that the intention behind them is to deceive. It is a matter for sober reflection that among all the bogus healings that are supposed to take place at Roman Catholic shrines such as Lourdes and Fatima, a core of real, indisputable cures takes place. In the same way, some of the manipulative charlatans on the fringes of the charismatic world who defraud gullible people with their counterfeit miracles can also lay claim to surprising successes. We have to reckon with the fact that our sovereign God permits Satan to exercise such power as part of the process of bringing judgement upon those who allow themselves to be duped by him.

This brings us to a consideration of the followers of Antichrist. A proportion of mankind will be taken in by his deception. As a consequence, they will perish. We have here a sobering description of how souls are lost (2:10-12) for what is true of those people who throw in their lot with the rebellion against God at the close of the age is also true of those who have defied God to his face throughout the whole of human history. Paul outlines a number of stages:

1. They do not 'receive the love of the truth' (2:10)

When the truth is presented to them, they have no welcome in their hearts for it, they spurn it. Over against this, they give an enthusiastic reception to **'the lie'** (2:11). While they will not entertain a miraculous Christ, they readily embrace the impostor. They discount the authentic signs and wonders recorded in the gospel, miracles intended to establish beyond doubt that Jesus Christ truly was all that he claimed to be, and they show a gullible, superstitious credulity in their uncritical acceptance of any display of supernatural power. Such a refusal to **'receive the love of the truth'** is not simply a failure on the intellectual level, as though the people in question had made an honest mistake. It goes hand in hand with taking **'pleasure in unrighteousness'** (2:12). People like that do not love the truth because they do love falsehood and wickedness.

2. They bring destruction upon themselves

The responsibility for all that follows rests squarely with the people concerned. Faced with a choice between God's truth and Satan's parody of it, they opted for deceit and sin rather than truth and goodness. God then confirms them in their chosen course of action by sending a **'strong delusion'** (2:11).

In verse 9 we read that **'the coming of the lawless one'** can be attributed to the restless energy of Satan. The devil, the father of lies, is the author of the cunning stratagems which are devised with the aim of deceiving his human victims. Nevertheless, at this point, Satan is merely the instrument used by the Almighty to accomplish his wider purposes. We must never think of Satan in such a way that we concede him a measure of independence of action. All of his activities, along with everything that ever comes to pass, fall within the scope of the sovereign purposes of God. The devil could attempt nothing against the patriarch Job without the express permission of the Lord (Job 1:12; 2:6). In the same way, the lying spirits who spoke through the mouths of Ahab's tame prophets in order to entice him to his death at Ramoth Gilead were sent by the Lord (1 Kings 22:22).

There is also an echo here of a subject which Paul treats in greater depth elsewhere (Rom. 1:18-32). The crux of it is that God is pleased to honour the moral choices of individuals. Those who embrace a particular lifestyle will eventually find that God gives them over to the consequences of their choice (Rom 1:24,26,28). Prefer lies to the truth of God and you will find yourself becoming hardened, increasingly willing to embrace a way of life which flaunts sin in its ugliest forms. One of the ways in which God punishes us for our sins is that he leaves us to wallow in them, allowing a dissipated lifestyle to take its inevitable toll upon us. Paul's stark message to his friends in Thessalonica was that those who deliberately indicate a liking for dubious philosophies and false systems of religion in preference to the truth of God will find that they become more and more enmeshed in the web of lies. It is as though God pronounces a doom upon them: 'Since that is what you wanted, that is what you shall have.' For certain people, no worse fate could be devised than to give them what they most want.

3. They ultimately perish

The process reaches its sickening conclusion when those who embrace error and moral evil are eventually condemned (2:12) and 'perish' (2:10). The human dupes of Antichrist will share the destiny of their figurehead. Like him (2:8), they will be destroyed. It is no trivial matter, then, to harden our hearts against the truth of God, to have no welcome for Jesus Christ, who is himself the truth. It is often the beginning of a downward slide which takes those who are on it with ever-quickening speed to the place of the damned. It is much the wiser policy to love the truth and take pleasure in righteousness.

15.
Paul's confidence in his friends

Please read 2 Thessalonians 2:13-17

Knowing that troubled times lay ahead, Paul urged the believers in Thessalonica to **'stand fast'** (2:15). Even as he did so, there was no doubt in his mind about the outcome. Paul wrote with serene confidence. His friends were made of the right stuff. They would pass the test. The reason for this solid confidence is revealed in his admission that he thanked God for his brothers and sisters (2:13-14). Indeed it is worth observing that he began his declaration of thanksgiving with the word **'But...'** He had just concluded a description of those who would not receive the love of the truth and who were on their way to hell because of it. What a relief to focus instead upon his brothers and sisters! Concentrate upon the destiny of those who reject God and we tremble. On the other hand, it is a joy to reflect on what will become of those who love Jesus. Why was Paul confident that everything would turn out well for the members of the church in Thessalonica? The heart of it all is the principle that when God sets out to save a person, a happy ending is never in doubt. In order to make this clear, the apostle provides us with an overview of the process of salvation which stretches from eternity in the past and reaches towards eternity in the future.

A comprehensive salvation (2:13-14)

1. God chooses those whom he saves

This choice dates **'from the beginning'**, namely the beginning of all things. Paul tells us elsewhere that 'before the foundation of the world' (Eph. 1:4), God determined whom he would save. The Almighty chose these people in order that he might save them. Christians often find this difficult to comprehend, partly because their own awareness of the grace of God began when they made a conscious decision to follow Jesus.

We ought to note in passing that God's choice of whom he would save is a sovereign act. 'He has mercy on whom he wills' (Rom. 9:18). It is sometimes argued that God chooses those who meet certain conditions. To be more specific, since he knows in advance who will repent of sin and turn to Christ, he chooses those very people. Although his choice of those people takes place before their decision to repent and believe the gospel, it is nevertheless dependent on it. This view of election robs the idea of God's choice of all meaning. It amounts to saying that the individuals in question leave God with no option but to choose them. In effect, it smuggles human merit into the process by claiming that believers deserved to be chosen because they met the required standard.

2. God sanctifies those whom he chooses

Having established that God chooses people in order that they might be saved, Paul went on to draw the attention of his friends in Thessalonica to two aspects of this salvation. In the first place, he reminded them that God the Holy Spirit initiates it all. He sanctifies those who believe. This means that he makes them holy. The word **'sanctification'** usually has two meanings in Scripture. The more common of the two is narrower in scope. It refers to the way that those who are already believers are helped to grow in grace. At this point, Paul uses the word in a wider, more general sense. The idea behind it is that a person is set apart for the service of God. In that sense, the whole process of salvation is involved.

There is more to salvation, however, than the activity of the Holy Spirit. If a person is to be saved, he or she must believe the truth of the gospel. While the latter cannot take place without the former, we must not allow the conviction that faith is God's gift to his chosen (Eph. 2:8) to obscure the fact that it is also an activity of the renewed nature. It is we who must believe. The Almighty does not believe for us or through us, but grants us by his Spirit the ability to do something that was formerly beyond our power. There is a deliberate contrast here between the followers of Antichrist and those who serve the true Christ. On the one hand, there are those who embrace lies and falsehood (2:11), while on the other, there are those who believe the truth. This is more than a commitment to truth in general. Ultimately it involves a commitment to Jesus Christ, who is himself the supreme expression and the embodiment of truth.

3. God calls his chosen at a particular moment in time

Even though God determined to set his love upon his chosen people before the universe itself came into being, they remain true to their nature and are 'children of wrath' like everybody else (Eph. 2:3) until they hear the summons that bids them take up the cross and follow Jesus. A young Chinese Christian once asked me to help him with a problem. 'Which is true', he wanted to know, 'do we choose Christ or does he choose us?' It is not a matter of choosing between alternatives. The one does not cancel out the other. All those who are chosen from eternity are called in time. No one else can respond to that call, for only those set apart by God the Spirit are able to decide for Christ. People like that would never dream of doing anything else!

The call of God comes through the presentation of the gospel. Many believers are aware that the Bible depicts God as the one who exercises control over the whole process of salvation. Nevertheless, they are troubled by their understanding of some of the implications. If God has already predetermined exactly whom he will save, does this not make evangelism a redundant, even a pointless activity? The answer is that the Lord has not only decided upon the identity of the people whom he intends to call, he has also settled the manner in which he means to do it! It is through the preaching of the gospel to every creature that the elect are called home to their preordained place near the heart of God. Suppose for a moment that this were not so and that everything hinged upon the response of individual men and women. If the outcome depends entirely upon the willingness of those who hear the gospel to turn to Christ and be saved, there is no more futile activity under heaven than evangelism. The only certainty is that the message will meet with wholesale rejection. If, on the other hand, it sometimes pleases God to add his own imperative summons to the entreaties of the preacher, evangelism becomes a stimulating and thrilling affair. Who can tell? Perhaps the next sermon that I preach will be God's instrument for bringing another of his people from darkness to light?

The outcome of the whole process is that those who are called in this manner 'obtain glory'. They eventually come to share in the splendour that surrounds the very being of God. Have you noticed that Paul sees the salvation of every Christian as a process which has its origin before the dawn of time and its conclusion in the far-distant reaches of eternity to come? By reminding his friends of the whole grand sweep of it, Paul intended them to grasp that no one is more secure than a Christian. From God's choice in eternity past, through his call in time and our believing response and then on to the endless ages of bliss which lie ahead, salvation is a grand design which is always brought to completion. None is chosen and called who is not subsequently glorified. If God has committed himself to you, he will not withdraw that commitment at some unspecified time in the future.

A stirring challenge (2:15)

This brings us to Paul's urgent plea that his brothers and sisters in Thessalonica should **'stand fast'**. At first sight, it might seem surprising that Paul wrote as he did. Given that the outcome was in the hands of God, surely nothing was required of the believers in Thessalonica other than to sit tight. God would see to it! The apostle, however, taught that the only fit response believers could make to the magnificent grace of God was, as John Wesley is reputed to have said, that they should be 'up and doing for Jesus'. There was work to be done. In particular, these first-century Christians should make it their business to see that whatever happened to others, they did not fall away. Paul described this in two ways. The tenacious believer will both 'stand fast' and **'hold'** tight, much as a man on board a ship in a howling gale would ensure that his feet were planted squarely on deck and that his arms were clutched tightly around a mast or a secure part of the rigging. In his letter to the Christians at Ephesus, Paul had spoken of those who are 'tossed to and fro and carried about with every wind of doctrine' (Eph. 4:14). There are still believers with no more spiritual stability than a scrap of litter whirling along the pavement in a stiff breeze.

How can we ensure that we do not end up like that? What a condemnation it would be if we were to resemble Jacob's son Reuben! The verdict on his life was that he was as 'unstable as water' (Gen. 49:4). Water is fluid; it has no shape of its own but alters to fit the shape of its container. In the same way, some Christians have an astonishing ability to merge with their surroundings.

The answer is to keep a firm grip on the 'traditions' that have been handed down to us. That word **'traditions'** has an important meaning. It refers to the truth that Paul had passed on because he in his turn had received it from God (see Gal. 1:11-12). There is a deliberate contrast here between Paul's behaviour and that of those who were troubling the Thessalonian Christians. They were circulating notions which they had cooked up for themselves; Paul had faithfully relayed a message that had its origin with God himself. Nowadays, certain religious traditions have gained widespread accept- ance but they are not what Paul had in mind for they are simply the ideas of men which have secured a place in the hearts of some worshippers because of their sheer antiquity. Paul was not making a plea that we cling to that which is merely old but rather that we cling to that which is authentic.

We need to exercise particular care when we refer to this matter of 'tradition' because of the important place that tradition occupies in Roman Catholicism. This is one of the things which makes it seem attractive. In recent years in the United Kingdom, there have been a number of high-profile conversions to Catholicism. Prominent figures, including senior politicians and minor royals, have switched allegiance from Protestantism to the church of Rome. It seems that one of the things which prompts such a change of course is the belief that the Protestant denominations, particularly the Church of England, offer an unseemly spectacle with senior clergymen not only disagreeing with the official position of their churches but also with one another. What does the Anglican Church stand for? It appears to stand for several contradictory views all at the same time. And a denomination which stands for everything at once really stands for nothing in particular.

Over against this situation where the Protestant bodies are gripped by an identity crisis, the Roman Catholic Church offers the reassuring sight of a body where, on the face of it, everyone believes the same thing and everyone holds the same convictions that have been held for centuries.

It is especially important, therefore, that we grasp that when the Roman church talks about tradition, it does not mean what Paul meant. The apostle envisaged a process where the truths which God had revealed were handed on from one generation of believers to another without being altered in transmission. For instance, in 2 Timothy 2:2 he asked Timothy to continue a process which he had already begun. He had received the truth from God and passed it on in turn to Timothy. Timothy would then transmit the same truth to other 'faithful men' who were gifted teachers and could relay the message to yet another generation of believers.

When Roman Catholic teachers refer to tradition they mean something quite different, an accumulated body of teachings which do not occur in the Bible but which have become so widely accepted that they are recognized as having the same validity as the truths contained in Scripture. For instance, the idea that the overwhelming majority of human beings go to a place called purgatory when they leave this world is a case in point. This notion has no biblical support whatever, yet it is a central plank in the Roman platform. In effect, tradition has become a rival source of authority to the Bible. Suppose someone were to ask, 'What should I believe? How should I live?' Roman Catholicism would encourage such a person to look at Scripture and tradition, notwithstanding the fact that many traditional beliefs held by Roman Catholics are actually contradicted by the Word of God.

To sum up, Paul's understanding was that tradition meant the faithful transmission of the teachings of Scripture, and that alone, from one generation to another, whereas the

Roman church has amassed a huge body of teachings and customs which disagree with the Bible and therefore undermine it.

It is of the utmost importance that we imitate the people whom Paul met in the Greek city of Berea, itself not far from Thessalonica. Their readiness to 'search the Scriptures' (Acts 17:11) tells us that they would only accept what Paul said when it was in harmony with what God had already said. To sum up then, the truth of God will keep us upright when the storms of controversy and doubt rage about us. Grasp hold of anything else and we have as much chance as a fairground balloon in a gale. The antidote to apostasy, to falling away, is a determined love for all that God has revealed in Scripture. Those people who stay the course are usually those who have steeped themselves in the Word of God. It is often said that the Bibles which are falling apart are usually owned by people who aren't!

A confident prayer (2:16-17)

As chapter 2 closes, the focus switches once more from the believer to his Lord. Once again we see Paul in prayer for his friends. His logic is impeccable. If they were to rise to the challenge which he had set, if they were to endure in the teeth of Satan's hostility, they would need help. So do we! The task is too big for us. It is not, however, beyond the power of God. In verse 17, Paul expressed the hope that he would **'establish'** his friends. This amounts to a prayer that God would give them that very quality of rock-like stability that he had set before the believers as a challenge. Without that help, they would surely fail. How encouraging then to see God portrayed as one who was committed to his people! Surely he who has loved his own and who has provided them with consolation that never fails and the hope of a bright future will supply the strength that they lack!

16.
Paul's request for prayer

Please read 2 Thessalonians 3:1-5

The previous chapter ended on a note of prayer as Paul expressed his desire that God would comfort and establish his readers (2:16-17). Now we see the apostle requesting prayer on his own behalf. That by itself would be enough to encourage them. It is all too easy to suppose that men with a distinguished record of service for God are so exalted that any help that ordinary believers might seek to give would be of no value. Surely Paul's gifts and personal qualities put him on a different plane from the average Christian! His request for prayer is therefore a reassuring indication that he did not regard himself as being beyond the need for help. He placed himself firmly in the category of those weak and sinful mortals who can accomplish nothing without the power of God. To sum up, Paul was not so great that he could manage without divine assistance and the Christians in Thessalonica were not so insignificant that they could not make a contribution to the success of his ministry.

So often when we seek the prayers of others, our chief concern is that they might plead with God to bless us by granting us good health or by easing our material circumstances. Paul's approach was different. Note that he urged his friends to pray for two things.

Prayer for the gospel

The apostle urged his friends to pray so that the message of salvation might have **'free course'** (3:1). This means that he longed to see it make rapid progress. In effect, the gospel is being compared to an athlete who has no obstacles in his path and is therefore able to run without being hindered.

The second part of his request, that the gospel should be **'glorified'**, refers to his longing that it might meet with an enthusiastic reception, that when people heard it they would honour it by responding positively to its demands.

All of this suggests that Paul's experience in Corinth had proved frustrating, which was in marked contrast to the way things had been when he first brought the message of the cross to Thessalonica. In his first letter Paul had spoken of the way that it had 'sounded forth' — it had rung out with the piercing clarity of a trumpet-call and to such effect that two whole provinces, Macedonia and Achaia, had felt the reverberations while the Thessalonians themselves had 'turned to God from idols to serve the living and true God, and to wait for his Son from heaven' (1 Thess. 1:8-10). Facing an uphill task in his efforts to make the truth known in Corinth, the apostle clearly longed for a measure of the impetus that he had experienced in Thessalonica.

Prayer for those who preach the gospel

Paul wanted his friends to pray that he and his missionary colleagues would be kept safe from malicious characters who tried to prevent the spread of the gospel by rendering the evangelists ineffective (3:2). Perhaps this has particular reference to the situation in Corinth, where Paul was the intended victim of a plot to incriminate him with the local authorities

(Acts 18:12-17). If so, it would seem that the prayers of his friends were answered for the case was heard by a man named Gallio, the proconsul of Achaia, who dismissed it as a frivolous waste of the court's time. Paul got safely away and the whole affair rebounded on the Jewish community in Corinth who were faced with an angry backlash from the Gentile majority.

It is important that we do not miss Paul's motive for asking his friends to pray that he and his fellow evangelists be kept out of trouble. No doubt the obvious consideration that it is never pleasant to be on the receiving end of physical violence or devious trickery was part of it all, but the success of the gospel was his overriding objective. If his message was to have 'free course', the evangelists would need to be able to get their message across unhindered.

Paul's confidence in God

Paul went on to speak of his confidence in God. He did so in two ways. First of all, there is a deliberate pun where he contrasted the faithlessness of his persecutors with the faithfulness of the Lord (3:2-3). You never really know where you are with the opponents of the gospel. They are fickle and unreliable. You cannot be certain of their reactions. The Lord, however, is dependable and can be relied upon to place his people on a firm footing and to protect them, not only from the malice of their human enemies, but also from the schemes of the devil who is at work behind the scenes.

Secondly, Paul observed that his confidence in God was such that he felt able to require certain things of them without any fear that his commands would be met with refusal (3:4). This was his way of preparing his readers for what was to follow, a passage where we see him in a very stern and unyielding frame of mind. How many of us would have phrased it as Paul did? Note that he did not say, 'I am confident that you will do all that I require.' That would have meant that his confidence was in them. He felt certain about the outcome for a different reason altogether. It was because God was at work in their lives.

17.
Paul's directions about the idle minority

Please read 2 Thessalonians 3:6-18

In verses 6-15 we see the apostle in a very determined mood. His language has a military feel to it, as though he were a drill sergeant on the parade ground. He issues commands (3:6,12), requires obedience (3:14) and refers to a certain element in the church at Thessalonica as **'disorderly'** (3:6,11), a word which actually referred to soldiers who were out of step, insubordinate and rebellious types who were not amenable to discipline.

Why did Paul adopt this brisk tone? The reason for it is that a problem which had arisen in the church at Thessalonica still persisted in spite of the fact that he had already addressed the matter in his previous letter (1 Thess. 4:9-12). (This is what Paul meant when he spoke in verse 6 of the **'tradition'** which they had already received from him.) The nature of the problem is clearly spelled out for us in verses 7 and 8 where Paul contrasts his own 'orderly' behaviour while he was there in person with the 'disorderly' conduct of this faction in the church. The apostle had been willing to earn his keep, to pay his own way, whereas this segment of the church membership were not.

It seemed that they excused their behaviour by pointing to the imminent return of the Lord Jesus: 'What's the point of working ourselves to the bone if Jesus is coming in a day or two?' The worst of it was that these people then took to sponging their meals from their brothers and sisters. Their treatment of their fellow-believers was far from loving. It involved unkindness on two levels. First of all, they stigmatized them as unspiritual and tried to persuade them to 'down tools' as well. Secondly, while all of this was going on, they felt no qualms about eating the food that their supposedly unspiritual brothers had paid for with the sweat of their brows.

In the meantime, the devil found work for their idle hands (3:11). Instead of being busy about their work, they were **'busybodies'**, poking their noses into other people's affairs and interfering in such a way as to make thorough nuisances of themselves.

Over the last two decades, certain British cities have witnessed vicious riots, usually in the areas where urban blight is at its worst. There has been a grim predictability about the responses of the politicians. The left inevitably blames it all on economic deprivation; the right argues that it is all down to human wickedness. Certainly it is a sinful act to loot a shop or set fire to a motor vehicle which belongs to someone else. The innate badness of the human heart must never be left out of the picture. But is it not equally true that people get up to far less mischief if they are usefully occupied? In the words of the old proverb, 'The devil finds work for idle hands.'

Paul's approach to the problem of the idle minority (3:6-15)

1. He reminded the church of his earlier teaching on the subject of work

During his stay in Thessalonica the apostle had insisted that '**If anyone will not work, neither shall he eat**' (3:10). There is an elementary justice about this. Who can quarrel with it?

2. He gave a decisive ruling

Having outlined the principle that believers should earn their own keep, Paul gave a sharp command to the people in question: let them earn their own living and stop causing trouble! (3:12).

3. He reminded the believers of the example he had set

He invited them to reflect on his own behaviour when he had been in Thessalonica (3:7-9). In the first letter he had cited the fact that he worked with his own hands in order to prove that he was not 'in it for the money', that he was not exploiting the goodwill of decent but gullible folk. In this second letter, his reason for mentioning his hard toil was essentially to shame the idlers in the church. He had far more right to eat the food from other people's tables than they! After all, he worked hard as a preacher of the gospel and had the right to live by it (1 Cor. 9:14), yet he had forgone that right in order to show them by example that hard work is part of the Christian's duty to his Master.

4. He demanded decisive action

What should be done if some of the idlers dug in their heels and simply refused to pay any attention to Paul's exhortation in verse 12? This would indicate a remarkable degree of stubbornness. It was not as if these people had not been told. To begin with, there is the strong possibility that they had been admonished by the elders of the church and had refused to accept the rebuke. Certainly Paul had felt it necessary to challenge the church about the attitude of some of its members towards the leadership (1 Thess. 5:12-14). This had been followed by Paul's own intervention in his first letter and now his much stronger treatment of the issue in the second. What can you do with people like that? Paul went on to propose a drastic remedy.

If we are to appreciate his reasons, it is important that we grasp the true nature of the offence. Here was a group of people who were refusing to heed the voice of Christ. They had been summoned to mend their ways by his appointed undershepherds who ruled in his name over the local church to which they belonged. They had compounded this refusal by being equally stiff-necked in the face of two warnings given by no less a figure than an apostle. Paul's words ought to have carried weight with them. They owed no less than their very conversion to him. In the face of this sheer unwillingness to yield an inch, Paul felt that the time had come to take decisive action. He therefore instructed the rest of the fellowship to withdraw from the people in question (3:14).

This step fell short of complete excommunication, that terrible step which churches are sometimes required to take when it becomes impossible to treat a person's profession of faith with any degree of credibility, whether because he or she has embraced heresy or a pattern of behaviour which gives the lie to the claim: 'Jesus has saved me from sin.' Paul clearly still thought of the people concerned as brothers (3:15). Nevertheless, they were brothers who had caused grave distress to the rest of the brotherhood. Perhaps it would bring them to their senses if the fellowship at large made its disapproval plain by maintaining a certain measure of reserve. It would, at the very least, invite them to ask themselves the question: 'Why do the other folk at church keep their distance from us?'

This leaves a question hanging in mid-air. What would Paul have advised if even this drastic step met with no response after a reasonable period of time? We can only conclude that a further step would be necessary, this time the complete exclusion of the person in question from all fellowship (see 1 Cor. 5:9-11).

When church discipline becomes necessary

Paul's approach to the 'idlers' at Thessalonica invites some reflections on the whole subject of church discipline. Firstly, it gives us some helpful guidance by providing an example of the kind of situation where such discipline becomes appropriate.

Two extremes can be observed in modern church life. On the one hand, there are those fellowships which will never act, no matter how flagrant the offence, while on the other horror stories abound about the excesses of those who go in for 'heavy shepherding'. It would seem that the leadership of some churches, despairing at the weakness of those situations where discipline is non-existent, have overbalanced in the opposite direction by exerting an intrusive measure of control over matters which are, properly speaking, the concern of no one but the individuals concerned. Incidentally, pastoral heavy-handedness of this kind is not confined to one style of churchmanship. It is by no means the exclusive province of extreme charismatic groups. I have heard of a church at one end of the evangelical spectrum which required all of its people to relocate to a different region of the country and another at the opposite end which insists that when members meet together in informal situations, they must never exceed a certain number.

In contrast to those who would do nothing and those who would intervene for trifling reasons, Paul stepped in because a serious breach of acceptable Christian standards warranted his doing so. When he took similar, if more drastic, action in Corinth, it was because of a case of sexual immorality which had become widely known. Likewise in Thessalonica, the behaviour of the unruly members who refused to work was an example of blatant disregard for the good of the fellowship as a whole. The idler who sponges off his brothers is engaging in a form of theft.

It is also worth noting the spirit which animated Paul's approach, a remarkable blend of firmness and gentleness. Christian standards must not be sacrificed, but at the same time, as long as some hope remained that brothers in Christ could be reclaimed for a position of usefulness and their credibility re-established, this should be kept in view.

Perseverance in doing good (3:13)

Few things can be so debilitating in the life of a local congregation as the sense that you are surrounded by people who do not share your level of loyal commitment. This is why Paul also encouraged the believers in Thessalonica not to **'grow weary in doing good'** (3:13). It is easy to imagine the sense of frustration that would have sapped the energies of conscientious church members who could see the idlers pursuing their policy of deliberate and sustained laziness. In such situations it is always tempting to give way to the 'Why should I bother?' syndrome. Do lazy church members ever reflect on the effect that they have on the fellowship at large? It is easy to feel disheartened by people who let everyone else do the work and leave you feeling that you have to bear a disproportionate share of the load. Those who never attend the prayer meeting or who support evangelistic ventures only once in a blue moon not only fall short themselves, they often leave a bitter legacy of betrayed hopes in the hearts of everyone else. Their friends have prayed again and again that they would do their fair share of the work, but 'Hope deferred makes the heart sick' (Prov. 13:12).

The problem of unemployment

As we conclude this section, it would be worth reminding ourselves that in one important respect, the situation in the developed Western economies of the late twentieth century is very different from the one which Paul knew. Nowadays, we face the terrible reality of mass unemployment. A combination of circumstances, from large-scale automation to the vagaries of market forces, has created a situation where the task of whittling down the huge total of the jobless seems almost intractable. Paul's brisk directive, 'If anyone will not work, neither shall he eat,' was not a first-century equivalent of that famously insensitive 'Get on your bike' remark made by a prominent politician in the early 1980s. The problem in Thessalonica was that certain people refused to take on work that was available. Some evangelical churches today have a very different problem — the pastoral needs of those who desperately want paid employment and have tried with might and main to get it, but whose efforts have been met with rejection after rejection. It is difficult to prevent the spirits flagging when the hundredth job application is met with a curt letter of rejection, or perhaps no letter at all. Nevertheless, it can help to recognize that 'work' and 'a job' are not one and the same thing. Certain jobs have little to be said in their favour except that they provide an income. The nature of the work involved is stultifying, doing nothing whatever to satisfy the creative instincts. Unemployed people need not be idle. While continuing to seek and pray for an opportunity to pay their own way in society, they can find imaginative ways of keeping busy. Many churches have benefited enormously from the hard work of members who, while out of paid work, have given sterling service to the life of their fellowships.

A word in closing (3:16-18)

This letter was dictated by Paul to a secretary. In order to guarantee that he was indeed the author, particularly in the light of bogus letters circulating among the churches which claimed to be from Paul (2:2), he concluded it with his own signature. There is also a final prayer for the apostle's friends, seeking two blessings in particular. First of all, there is **'peace'**. Paul's expression is wonderfully comprehensive. He asked God to grant them peace all the time and in every situation. This depends in its turn upon **'the grace of our Lord Jesus Christ'**. It is because God is kind to the undeserving, especially in the gift of a Saviour to an unresponsive and uncaring world, that peace in the heart is a real possibility. The person who knows that God has no quarrel with him has every reason to be calm in his soul.

Appendix I
A word about the last things

I grew up in a large industrial town in the north-east of England and became a Christian during my teens. I attended an evangelical church there and was a regular at the weekly young people's meeting. One January night, the meeting had just closed and a noisy throng of young people spilled out of the chapel onto the pavements. It was one of those nights when the air is clear and cold. The sky was as black as ink and the stars were spangled across it in riotous profusion. We soon fell silent at the grandeur of it. A friend came up to me, and overwhelmed by the brilliance of the night sky said, 'Wouldn't it be great if the Lord were to come back now?' As it happened, the monthly deacons' meeting had concluded at the same time as our Young People's Fellowship and a veteran believer had overheard my friend's remark. 'It can't happen yet, son,' he said. 'They haven't rebuilt the temple in Jerusalem!' As well as doing a great deal to spoil a lovely moment, this observation alerted me for the very first time to the fact that Christians are not all of one mind about the events which will accompany our Lord's return. I had assumed that if the phrase 'thief in the night' meant what it said, the Second Coming would be completely unexpected and that tomorrow morning might well be the last to dawn upon our tired planet. But here was a man who thought that a building project in Palestine would provide a measure of warning before the end came.

Since that time, I have come to appreciate that the issues are vastly more complex than I could have imagined. Christians who read and love the same Bible, and who depend upon it to shape all their convictions about God and his dealings with mankind, nevertheless manage to arrive at different conclusions on this subject. All are convinced that Christ is surely coming, but there are differences of opinion about the manner and the timing of his coming as well as the events which will surround it.

A survey of different views of the last things

The different schools of thought take their names from the attitude they adopt to the 'millennium', the period of one thousand years described in Revelation 20:1-6. What follows is a brief outline of each position. At this point, a note of caution is required. Each position is itself a wide spectrum of opinion. Within each camp, scholars will disagree over matters of detail.

I have deliberately refrained from giving comprehensive Scripture proofs for each viewpoint. Those who want to find out how scholars have arrived at their conclusions would be best advised to consult some of the numerous books available in defence of each position! I have also purposely avoided passing comment and have contented myself with simply describing the different views. Readers must study the Scriptures for themselves and decide in the light of their study where the relative strengths and weaknesses of each position lie.

1. Premillennialism

This is the view that Christ will return before the millennium. Most premillennialists would believe something roughly in line with the following outline:

1. Towards the end of world history the suffering and persecution of believers will climax in the rise of Antichrist.

2. When Antichrist is at the height of his power, Christ will appear to triumph over all his enemies, resurrect the saints and establish his kingdom on earth, which will last for a thousand years and during which Jerusalem will be rebuilt and righteousness and peace will reign. (It is only fair to add that some think in terms of a literal thousand years, whereas others would take it as a symbol referring to a lengthy period which turns out, in the purposes of God, to be just right.)

3. At the end of this period, the unbelieving dead will be raised for the final judgement.

4. God will call the new heavens and the new earth into being and inaugurate the 'final state'.

2. *Dispensationalism*

Premillennialism is a viewpoint which has been held throughout the history of the Christian church. Dispensationalism is a variety of it which came to prominence in the early decades of the nineteenth century. When I first became a Christian, most of the believers I knew were convinced that it represents the teaching of Scripture. While not as popular among British evangelicals as it was half a century ago, it still has many adherents. I understand that it still has a considerable following in the United States. Dispensationalists are far from unanimous about the precise details of their scheme, but a typical outline would be as follows:

1. God has revealed that human history will pass through seven distinct phases, or dispensations (hence the name 'dispensationalism'). These are 'Innocency' (from the creation of the world to the Fall), 'Conscience'

(from the Fall to the Flood), 'Human government' (from
the Flood to the destruction of the Tower of Babel),
'Promise' (from the patriarchs to Moses), 'Law' (from
Moses to Christ), 'Grace' (from the first coming of
Christ to the advent of the millennium) and 'Kingdom'
(the period of the millennium itself). Some dispen-
sational scholars have also argued that the seven
churches in Revelation chapters 2 and 3 portray the
spiritual condition of the people of God in each of the
seven dispensations.

2. The nation of Israel occupies a special place in the
purposes of God. It was the provisional form of the
kingdom of God. Because of apostasy, it was over-
thrown, but the prophets predicted that it would be re-
established. The Messiah came and offered to re-estab-
lish this kingdom, but as the Jews refused, this has been
postponed until the coming of the millennial kingdom.

This means, in effect, that the church is a parenthesis
in the history of the kingdom. The gospel of grace for the
nations is a windfall which has resulted from the apostasy of Israel.

3. Christ's second coming will consist of two separate events. First of all, he will come for his saints. The
saints will be caught up to meet the Lord in the air. This
is often viewed as a 'secret rapture'. Unbelievers will
simply awake one morning to the disconcerting realization that their Christian neighbours have vanished. A
period of seven years will then elapse, during which the
gospel of the kingdom will again be preached (by
believing Jews), many will be converted and towards
the end of this period, Antichrist will be revealed and
God's wrath will be poured out upon the human race.
After this period, Christ will come with his saints. The
nations will be judged, the saints who died during the

great tribulation will be raised up, Antichrist will be destroyed and Satan bound.

4. The millennial kingdom will then be established. It will be an earthly, visible kingdom in which the Jews only will be natural citizens; the Gentiles will be adopted citizens. Christ will sit on a throne in Jerusalem. The temple will be rebuilt and animal sacrifices offered once more. Universal peace and prosperity will reign and a large proportion of mankind converted.

5. At the end of the millennium Satan will be loosed for a short period, his 'little season'. Gog and Magog will rise against the holy city, but God will intervene with fire from heaven. Satan will be cast into the pit and the unbelieving dead will now, at last, be resurrected to appear before the judgement seat of God.

6. Then will follow the eternal kingdom of heaven.

3. Postmillennialism

This is the view that Christ will return after the millennium. Many evangelical postmillennialists believe something along these lines:

1. The Holy Spirit will gradually bring about the virtual triumph of true Christianity before Christ returns.

2. Some believe that a great apostasy will take place before this 'golden age'; others believe that it will follow it. Among those who believe that the apostasy will take place beforehand, there are many who think that the papacy at its height was the great apostasy. It follows that the Reformation began the course of events which will, in time, bring about the millennium.

3. Christ will return after the world is evangelized, the Jews converted and the church brought to a position of great influence, purity and unity.

4. This will be followed by the general resurrection, that is to say, that all the dead, believers and unbelievers alike, will be raised at the same time.

5. This will be followed in turn by the general judgement.

6. Then the eternal kingdom will begin.

4. *Amillennialism*

This view, also known as non-millennialism, supposes that there is no literal millennium but rather that the millennium is a symbolic term used to describe the period between Christ's first and second comings. In other words, we do not so much await a future millennium as live in the millennium right now. Most amillennialists also believe that tribulation and blessing will be the present experience of Christians throughout the world. Neither is confined exclusively to one period of history or another. It follows that believers need to be on their guard against the possibility of trial and testing because Satan is malicious, but there are also grounds for optimism because God is generous. Most amillennialists anticipate something like this:

1. The forces of good and evil will both develop side by side.

2. Some believe that there will be tribulation and apostasy throughout this era, whereas others expect that it will be concentrated in time immediately before the return of Christ.

3. Some believe that there will be no sign that Christ's return is imminent, whereas others expect:

a. The great apostasy, concentrated in time just prior to the end.

     b. The conversion of the Jews.

     c. A state of affairs in which it can be said that
the gospel has been preached to all the nations.

    4. Christ will return, whereupon the general resurrection of the dead, believers and unbelievers alike, will take place.

    5. The general judgement will follow.

    6. The new heaven and the new earth will appear, to last for ever.

In conclusion

With the exception of dispensationalism, each of these schools of thought has a long pedigree. For most of the last two thousand years, Christian people have been attracted to each view of the last things. Moreover, eminent servants of God have been far from unanimous. Each point of view can number great preachers, theologians and missionaries among its champions. At the very least, this should encourage us to be cautious. If fine Christians who have known the blessing of God upon their lives and who have loved the same Saviour and the same Bible have not seen eye to eye on the matter, we for our part must learn to accept those who differ from us. Individual Christians, as well as local churches, denominations and theological seminaries, have been much too ready to divide over the issue amid accusations of heresy.

    I once heard about a conference where the subject of the last things was the main item on the programme. The conference hall was a regular rabbit-warren of a building, with a labyrinth of corridors and staircases. When the coffee-break arrived, the chairman asked the premillennialists, post-millennialists and amillennialists to assemble at the serving point by different routes. He concluded by saying, 'Please observe that you will all arrive at the same place, at the same time!'

Surely we are all agreed on this much at least, that 'Christ is surely coming, bringing his reward.' 'Amen. Even so, come, Lord Jesus!' (Rev. 22:20).

Appendix II
A word about books

The book which you have just read began its life as a set of notes for my own use as I conducted the mid-week Bible studies at Free Grace Baptist Church in Lancaster. At that early stage in their existence they had a modest and rather limited purpose. Our Bible studies are interactive. Discussion ranges far and wide and it can sometimes be enormously tempting to wander off down any one of a number of promising byways which open up before us as the evening unfolds. I like to have notes before me as a prompt to prevent my wandering too far away from the passage before us. A modest set of notes has now grown into a modest book, an attempt to provide a straightforward explanation of 1 and 2 Thessalonians for the benefit of the ordinary Christian. (Pedantic readers might want to insist that since every believer has experienced a life-changing encounter with the Son of God, no Christian can fairly be described as 'ordinary', but I'm sure that you know what I mean!) I would be thrilled if this little book has encouraged you to dig deeper. In that case, there are a number of other books which you might like to add to your collection.

First of all, Geoffrey B. Wilson has written a number of books on the epistles of Paul. He has called them *Digests of Reformed Comment*. Each one takes the reader through the epistle in question, looking at each verse in turn. Instead of commenting on the verses himself, Mr Wilson has gathered a selection of quotations from the works of great Bible scholars. Although these books are small, and therefore attractively priced, they are crammed with good things. Serious Bible students ought to consider acquiring not only the volume on 1 and 2 Thessalonians, but the entire set. It would be money well spent. These books are produced by the Banner of Truth Trust.

Inter Varsity Press have published two helpful titles: one is in *The Bible Speaks Today* series and was written by John R. W. Stott; the other is in their series of Tyndale Commentaries and is by Dr Leon Morris.

Dr Morris has also written a more 'heavyweight' commentary as part of the *New International Commentary on the New Testament* series, published by Eerdmans. I found both works by Dr Morris to be extremely helpful. The second of the two is both larger and more demanding.

Time spent reading anything written by William Hendriksen is always time well spent. A copy of his commentary on 1 and 2 Thessalonians, published by the Banner of Truth Trust, would be a good investment.

The prayers of Paul are a fascinating study in their own right. D. A. Carson has written a book entitled *A Call to Spiritual Reformation*. This book, published by Inter Varsity Press, is an exposition of a number of the prayers of the great apostle, including those found in 1 and 2 Thessalonians. I can say without the slightest reservation that it is one of the most challenging books I have ever read. If you only have time to read one book in the next twelve months, buy or borrow this one and read it!

Books on the last things are available in huge numbers. Some combine wild speculation with the style of a tabloid newspaper and are best left alone. Naturally, every author who writes on this subject will soon give the game away about which school of interpretation he prefers. For my part, I confess to being an amillennialist. If that hasn't put you off, let me recommend three titles which will provide a helpful introduction to this area of Christian doctrine. The first two are published by Banner of Truth. They are *The Momentous Event* by W. J. Grier and *The Last Things* by Paul Helm. I place enormous value on my third recommendation, *The Bible on the Life Hereafter* by William Hendriksen, published by Baker Book House. This little book charts a path through a complex area of teaching. Each chapter is written as the answer to the kind of questions which many believers ask about Christ's return and the world to come.

Finally, you may have come across the disturbing news that some evangelical scholars now question the doctrine of the eternal punishment of those who reject Christ and his salvation. Several helpful books have been written in response to this development. One which is thorough, readable and compelling is *Whatever happened to Hell?*, by John Blanchard, published by Evangelical Press.

Christ is surely coming,
Bringing his reward,
Alpha and Omega,
First and last and Lord;
Root and stem of David,
Brilliant morning star,
Meet your Judge and Saviour,
Nations near and far!
Meet your Judge and Saviour,
Nations near and far!

See the holy city!
There they enter in,
Men by Christ made holy,
Washed from every sin:
Thirsty ones desiring
All he loves to give,
Come for living water,
Freely drink and live!
Come for living water,
Freely drink and live!

Grace be with God's people!
Praise his holy name!
Father, Son and Spirit,
Evermore the same.
Hear the certain promise
From the eternal home:
'Surely I come quickly!' —
Come, Lord Jesus, come!
'Surely I come quickly!' —
Come, Lord Jesus, come!

Christopher Idle (1938-).